Thérèse of Lisieux

THÉRÈSE OF LISIEUX

by Joan Monahan

Paulist Press
New York/Mahwah, N.J.

COVER ART AND INTERIOR ILLUSTRATIONS BY PATRICK KELLEY

COVER DESIGN BY LYNN ELSE

Library of Congress Cataloging-in-Publication Data

Monahan, Joan, 1926–
    St. Thérèse of Lisieux / by Joan Monahan.
        p. cm.
    Summary: A biography of the nineteenth-century French Carmelite who wrote of a path to Heaven, "The Little Way," that can be followed by ordinary Christians and who was canonized a saint just seventeen years after her death at age twenty-four.
    ISBN 0-8091-6710-7 (alk. paper)
    1. Thâeráese, de Lisieux, Saint, 1873–1897—Juvenile literature. 2. Christian saints—France—Lisieux—Biography—Juvenile literature. 3. Lisieux (France)—Biography. [1. Thâeráese, de Lisieux, Saint, 1873–1897. 2. Saints. 3. Women—Biography.] I. Title: Saint Thérèse of Lisieux. II. Title
BX4700. T5 M62 2003
282'.092—dc21

                                                                                    2003001685

Published by Paulist Press
997 Macarthur Boulevard
Mahwah, New Jersey 07430

www.paulistpress.com

Printed and bound in the
United States of America

TABLE OF CONTENTS

*To the O'Malley family for their generous love
through the years*

Acknowledgments

To Susan Heyboer O'Keefe for her helpful and gracious editing. To Kathy Riley for sharing her many resources on St. Thérèse. And to all those who provided helpful commentary on the text.

INTRODUCTION

St. Thérèse of the Child Jesus and the Holy Face, a nineteenth-century French Carmelite, died when she was only twenty-four. She brings to those who follow her "Little Way" a fresh approach to holiness, illuminating a path to heaven attainable by ordinary Christians. Unlike other saints, she performed no miracles during her earthly life, experienced no astonishing revelations, and performed no exceptional penances. Her life was instead characterized by her profound love of God, which led her to understand with astonishing clarity the words of scripture. Consequently she abandoned herself wholeheartedly to Jesus and embraced her final sufferings with absolute joy.

Her influence has swept like a meteor across the skies. Shortly before she died, she wrote to a Carmelite missionary whom she called her brother that she planned to continue working in heaven for God "to make Him loved by a multitude of souls who will bless Him eternally." Her intercessionary activity was felt within just a few years of her death as her autobiography, *The Story of a Soul,* was eagerly passed from hand to hand. At first intended only for those few people who were close to her, this little book has circled the world and been translated into at least fifty-six languages.

This present biography is a small attempt to capture the spirit of this young woman whose heavenly influence continues to be felt daily. A most extraordinary girl who insisted that she was most ordinary, Thérèse has captured the hearts of all those who have discovered her, whether deliberately or by accident. Her attraction is wide-ranging and appeals to everyone from the person in the pew to the popes.

In 1914, just seventeen years after her death, Pius X called her in private "the greatest saint of modern times." Benedict XV exempted her from the normal wait of fifty years required before canonization. Pius XI called her "the cherished child of the world" and made her "the star of his pontificate" as he beatified her in 1923 and canonized her just two years later. Pius XII named her Secondary Patroness of France, equal to her heroine, St. Joan of Arc, and called her "the greatest wonder-worker of modern times." Although Thérèse is not mentioned in the official documents of Vatican II, her influence is clear to scholars. Not the least of these influences is her reaffirmation of the call to sanctity to all the baptized. And finally, in 1997, just a hundred years after her death, John Paul II named her a Doctor of the Church because of the wisdom of her teachings, one of only three women to be so named. Since that time, her relics have been honored by millions of people in tours to twenty-two countries.

Thérèse's teaching is deceptively simple. We are to become as little children, trusting in our heavenly

Father to fulfill all our needs and loving him with the everlasting love with which he has loved us. Given the grace to love God early in life, she understood and practiced the words of Christ: "Truly I tell you, unless you change and become like children, you will never enter the kingdom of heaven. Whoever becomes humble like this child is the greatest in the kingdom of heaven" (Matt 18:3–4). This is the core of her "Little Way": to follow this path of love and to accept freely the suffering and trials of daily living. Cardinal Paul Poupard, speaking at ceremonies marking the centennial observance of her death, said that Thérèse teaches that our interior life is not measured by any extraordinary human actions but by "the love of God made known in our hearts."

If this book can lead at least one person to answer Thérèse's final prayer and become one of the legions of those who will follow her "Little Way," it will have served its purpose.

CHAPTER ONE

A HOLY FAMILY

As a mother comforts her child,
so I will comfort you.
Isaiah 66:13

To understand St. Thérèse of Lisieux, it is necessary to see her in the cradle of her family, the adored ninth and last child of Zélie and Louis Martin, growing up in late nineteenth-century France. To be a child nurtured by these parents and surrounded by the love of four older sisters was the comfort that God gave Thérèse as a young child. Her mother prayed often for one of her children to be a saint, a priest, or a missionary. In Thérèse, her prayers were answered.

The Parents of Thérèse

Zélie and Louis were remarkable parents. They were declared *venerable* in 1994, which means they themselves are on the path to beatification by the church.

Before their marriage, Thérèse's mother and father had each hoped to live as a religious, although that was to be neither one's true vocation. As a young man, Louis Martin had applied to become a Canon in the Great Saint Bernard Hospice high in the Swiss Alps. He was refused entrance until he could gain greater knowledge of and fluency in Latin. He hired a tutor and began this difficult work. After a year and a half, he gave up this study and concentrated on becoming a watchmaker. When he returned to the city of Alençon, he bought a house and opened a shop for watchmaking and repair and brought his parents to live with him. His days were filled with daily Mass, prayer, work, study, and occasional hunting and fishing trips. Although he joined the Catholic Circle, a group of single young men and women, he had little interest in meeting young women or in socializing.

At thirty-four, Louis was prosperous and had purchased a plot of land just outside the city. A statue of Mary had a place of honor in this garden. In all, it was a perfect place for the solitude, prayer, and reflection that was so important to him. But he was still single, and his mother was concerned. While she was attending a class on lacemaking, she met an attractive young Christian girl, Zélie, who was gifted at lacemaking, for which Alençon was noted.

Like Louis, Zélie had also been attracted to religious life and had applied to the Sisters of Saint Vincent de Paul. The sisters did not believe her vocation was to religious life. They did think, however, that she would make a wonderful Christian mother. In a letter to her sister, Marie-Louise, who was already a Visitation sister, Zélie wrote, "So I'll get married and have a lot of children." But whatever vocation she followed, she noted that she wanted to be a saint.

Meanwhile, she had opened her own shop for lace-making. She created intricate designs for lacework and soon had about twenty young women working for her making the individual pieces. Zélie would then assemble the separate pieces to make the finished product, which might be anything from a lace collar or cuffs to a tablecloth. The assembly work was the most difficult part because the pieces had to be connected in such a way that the connections could not be seen. Zélie was very skillful at this assembly work.

It was not long after Mme. Martin's discovery of Zélie that the Martin and Guérin families arranged a meeting between the two. Such arrangements were common at that time. Soon Zélie and Martin discovered their "similar inclinations," and plans were made for their marriage. Just three months after their first meeting, the twenty-seven-year-old Zélie and the thirty-five-year-old Louis were married on July 13, 1858. As was customary at that time, the wedding was held at midnight in the Church of Notre Dame in Alençon.

Soon afterwards, the couple resolved to live as brother and sister. They decided their marriage would model itself on the union of St. Joseph and the Blessed Virgin. For ten months the marriage was patterned on this holy ideal. Young women of this time were not as knowledgeable as young women today, and so the innocent Zélie did not understand that this arrangement prevented her from becoming a mother. A confessor suggested to the couple that their responsibility in marriage was to bear children. And so they did.

The Children of Louis and Zélie

Their first child was born in 1860 and was named Marie. All of the Martin children would be given this first name, even the boys, a practice common in Catholic countries with a devotion to Mary. But the Martins' devotion was deeply personal as well. The statue of Mary that had graced Louis's retreat was now in their home. Evening prayers were said together before it.

The first girl was the only one actually called by the name Marie. A year later Pauline was born and two years after that, Léonie. A year later, in 1864, Hélène was born. By this time, Zélie was suffering from a breast tumor and was becoming unable to nurse her children herself. Hélène's birth was followed in 1866 by a boy named Marie Joseph Louis, who lived only five months. In 1868, a second boy was born. He was baptized Marie Joseph Jean-Baptiste, but he lived only eight months. Children at the end of the nineteenth century had a high mortality rate, so such deaths were not unusual. In addition, Zélie's inability to nurse these later children made them easy prey for intestinal trouble. The deaths of the two boys, and also of Zélie's parents during the same time, brought the family much pain.

The following year, in 1869, Céline was born. However, this joy was soon diminished in 1870 by the death of little Hélène, just five and a half years old, followed by the birth and death of Mélanie Thérèse. But Zélie was optimistic and when she became pregnant again, she wrote, "I'm crazy about children; I was born to have them." She felt that *this* baby was especially strong and happy. When she sang, she thought the baby sang with her. If the new baby were to be a girl, she planned to name it Thérèse in honor of Teresa of Avila and in memory of Mélanie Thérèse.

Despite her health problems and her growing family, Zélie continued her successful lacemaking business. The business was doing so well that in 1870 Louis sold his watchmaking shop and took over management of Zélie's business affairs. Louis Martin, who enjoyed traveling, was able to travel to Paris to promote Zélie's lacework and obtain new orders. Zélie was working long hours, and she said she felt "enslaved." On Thursdays she would see clients, and on other days she was busy joining the delicate pieces of lace together to fill "the orders which keep coming in and do not give me a moment's rest." Still the Martins were a happy and close-knit family. Zélie remarked, "My husband is a saintly man; I wish all women could have one just like him." Even with the children and business activities, there was still always time for daily morning Mass, evening prayer, and other devotions.

At this time, the Franco-German War swirled around the Martin family, and Alençon was in danger of invasion. For a short while they had to lodge nine Prussian soldiers in their home. Fortunately, in 1871, the family moved to a larger home with a garden and there, once the soldiers were gone, they were content to stay, even refusing invitations that would interrupt the peaceful flow of their lives.

The Birth and Early Days of Thérèse

On January 2, 1873, the child who would become the darling of her parents and her four living sisters was born. Two days later she was baptized and christened Marie-Françoise-Thérèse in the Church of Notre Dame where her parents had married. Her godparents were her oldest sister, Marie, and Paul-Albert Boul, the son of a friend of Louis Martin. Although both were only thirteen, they took seriously the duties of godparenting.

Thérèse immediately charmed the family and appeared to be a happy, healthy baby, "always cheerful" according to Zélie. Still, Zélie could not nurse her. By February, Thérèse seemed to lose ground, suffering the same intestinal problems that had caused the death of her siblings. The doctor warned Zélie that someone would have to be found to nurse Thérèse if she was to survive.

Louis was not home, so Zélie herself set off for the home of Rose Taillé, who had nursed the two Martin baby boys. Rose, her husband, and her four young sons lived in a small rural community a short distance from Alençon. Rose returned with Zélie and remained for eight days. At first they were not sure the baby would live, but she soon responded. Since Rose could not remain away from her own family too long, Thérèse moved with Rose to the country.

Thérèse Becomes a Country Girl

Thérèse quickly adjusted to country life and to the beliefs and customs of the Taillé family—such as protecting the cricket who sang at their hearth because it was supposed to bring them good luck. Another custom involved flowers. Flowers grew in abundance and were shared with friends and neighbors at every possible occasion. No doubt this helped bring about Thérèse's love of flowers. She also enjoyed playing with Rose's four boys. They took her on rides in a wheelbarrow filled with hay. She would be perched on top of the family cow, Redskin, and held there for a special ride. Soon Zélie was to write of her, "She became a big baby browned by the sun."

The separation from her youngest daughter was difficult, but Zélie knew it was necessary for Thérèse's health. Fortunately, the separation was not total, and Zélie and her other daughters—Marie, Pauline, Léonie, and Céline—often traveled to the countryside to see the baby. They would bring city food, like white bread, to share with the Taillés, and in return enjoyed the black bread, fruits, and vegetables that were part of country fare.

Also, each week on Thursday, Rose would go into the city to sell her butter, eggs, and other products at the market. She would attempt to leave little Thérèse with her mother at that time, but Thursdays were the days when Zélie had many visitors, both lacemakers and wealthy customers. Often Thérèse would cry until it was necessary to take her to Rose at the market to quiet her. There Thérèse would sit happily for the rest of the day.

Soon Zélie discovered that Thérèse was not afraid of the laceworkers, because they were simple girls like Rose. It was the wealthy customers dressed in their fancy clothes and large feathered hats who terrified her. Eventually Thérèse learned to play with her sister Céline, who was just a few years older. When she was with Céline, she would pull herself up by a chair and stand on her wobbly legs. Zélie saw Thérèse grow in health each week and laugh with joy as she played with Céline. The deep friendship between the two sisters developed early.

Soon it would be time for the baby to return to her city home. When Thérèse was fourteen months old, she moved back to Alençon. To prepare for her return, Zélie made a "sky-blue dress, little blue shoes, a blue sash, and a pretty white bonnet." It was a day of celebration. Although leaving Rose must have been a hardship for Thérèse, Zélie found her to be "very sweet and advanced for her age."

Reflection

Thérèse wrote of these early days, "God was pleased all through my life to surround me with love, and the first memories I have are stamped with smiles and the most tender caresses! But although He placed so much love near me, He also sent much love into my little heart, making it warm and affectionate."

Love was the cornerstone of Thérèse's life. We should try to make both the receiving of love from our Lord, our family, our friends, even acquaintances, and the giving of love to all in return the cornerstone of our own lives.

St. Thérèse, stir up in our hearts the fire of love.

CHAPTER TWO

EARLY CHILDHOOD IN ALENÇON

*In the shadow of your wings
I sing for joy.*
Psalm 63:7

After almost a year with Rose, her nurse, Thérèse came home to her family and quickly found her special place as the youngest and last of the Martin children. This golden-haired, gray-eyed child learned how to give and receive love generously from all members of her family. These years, until she was almost five, Thérèse remembered as being the happiest of her life. She says of this time, "Oh! Everything truly smiled upon me on this earth: I found flowers under each of my steps." Since these early years have much to do with the character formation of an individual, it is helpful to observe Thérèse as a developing youngster.

In her autobiography, *The Story of a Soul*, Thérèse relates many stories of these early days. Her memory was strengthened, no doubt, by things her mother told her and by the many letters her mother wrote, especially to Thérèse's older sisters, Marie and Pauline, who were at boarding school in the Visitation Convent of Le Mans, returning home only in summer and for holidays.

Religious Devotion in the Home

During this time, much of France was either anticlerical or infected with the heresy of Jansenism, which argued that only a few are chosen for heaven and that predestination is absolute. Yet the Martins were remarkable for their joyful attention to all kinds of religious observances. Holidays in this family were true holy days. M. and Mme. Martin attended daily Mass, as did Marie and Pauline when they were home from school. Evening devotions closed their days, and during the day the family never seemed to lose sight of the presence of God in their lives.

Once when Marie had put Thérèse into a cold bed without making her say her prayers, the little girl protested the cold bed, but more than that, she protested that she hadn't said her prayers. When Marie finally finished her own prayers and climbed into the now warm bed, Thérèse was still complaining that she hadn't said her prayers.

The family often remembered in prayer the four Martin children who had died. The death of Hélène, only five at her death, particularly haunted Zélie Martin. Not only did she mourn the child's death, but she also was concerned about the child's eternal future. Zélie had not taken Hélène to confession, although she knew the child had told a white lie shortly before her death. Zélie worried that Hélène was suffering in purgatory because of her mother's neglect. Obsessed with anxiety, Zélie turned to the statue of Our Lady for comfort. (This statue was an important figure in the Martin household. The fingers had been damaged by the frequent kisses placed there by various family members.) While praying, Zélie heard an interior voice assuring her that Hélène was in heaven beside Our Lady. With this assurance, Zélie was able to cast her worries aside and rejoice. Both the devotion to the Blessed Mother that had worn the statue's fingers away, and Zélie's concern that she might be responsible for her little girl's detention in purgatory, were typical of the deep piety of the household.

Céline and Thérèse

During these early years Thérèse was an unusually happy child. Her friendship with her sister, Céline, blossomed. In fact, the two were almost inseparable. Thérèse wanted always to be with Céline. For example, after supper she would demand to be released from her high chair in order to go to play with her big sister who had finished first. This often meant she would have to forgo her dessert, but being with Céline was more important. Sometimes play would take them outside, but at other times they would sit before the fireplace enjoying their pet chickens. Nurse Rose had given Thérèse a rooster and a chicken, and Thérèse, in turn, had given the rooster to Céline.

The garden was a special place for play. The two would play wolf, blow bubbles, and even climb small trees. They particularly enjoyed a swing that their father had put up in the garden for them. As the youngest, Thérèse had to be tied into the swing so that she could go as high as she wished without falling. And she always wanted to go higher.

When Marie would come to take Céline for her beginning lessons, Thérèse would cry unless she was permitted to follow along. Attending the lesson would mean she would have to sit quietly for two or three hours. To keep her occupied, Marie would give her some beads to thread or a small scrap of material for sewing. Thérèse would not dare to interrupt Marie during the lesson, and if her needle became unthreaded it was a small tragedy. She would try to rethread the needle, a hopeless task for small fingers, and she would finally melt into quiet tears. Marie, seeing her distress, would rethread the needle for her, and the lesson would continue, with Thérèse smiling through her tears.

Though neither of these two little girls was yet ten years old, they often had spiritual discussions. One day Céline questioned how God could be present in the small host. Thérèse answered, "That is not surprising; God is all powerful."

"What does all powerful mean?" Céline asked.

"It means he can do what he wants."

A Complex and Interesting Personality Develops

Thérèse was a happy child, but spirited as well. She could be patient while waiting for Céline to finish her lessons, but she could be persistent in getting her way. When a childish disagreement happened while playing with Céline, it would be Céline who would give in to Thérèse. Céline had learned what their mother had noted: "Thérèse is not as gentle as Céline and has an almost unconquerable stubborn streak in her; when she says no, nothing can make her give in, and you can put her in the cellar for the day and she would rather sleep there than say yes."

When frustrated or denied something she felt should be hers, she often resorted to tantrums. Such stubbornness of character can be a defect or a strength. Thérèse, with the help of her parents and sisters, would develop it as a strength.

Once when she was only two, she did not attend Mass with the family. Later she set off in the rain for church by herself because she had missed "Matt." The nanny, Louise, who cared for Céline and Thérèse, had to run to church after her, capture her, and return her, screaming, to her home. Thérèse felt that Louise favored Céline and later wrote that she was pleased that this was so because, as she noted, "Otherwise I would have been frightfully spoiled."

On another occasion, to test the willfulness and pride of Thérèse, her mother told her that if she would kiss the floor, she would be given a sou. A sou is worth about a nickel, a small fortune for a little girl in those days. In response, Thérèse drew her small frame up as tall as she could and announced, "I would prefer not to have the sou."

But when things were given to her as gifts, she accepted them with enthusiasm. When Léonie was about thirteen, she decided she was too old for dolls and making doll dresses, so she brought her doll, some dresses, and a basketful of scraps of fabrics, ribbons, and lace, saying, "Here, my little sisters, choose. I'm giving you all of this." Céline reached for a ball of yarn, but Thérèse took all the rest, saying, "I choose all." Later, as a Carmelite, this trait would show itself as Thérèse accepted with an absolute trust in Jesus all that was offered to her. What might be seen as selfishness developed into an openness of spirit. Thérèse wanted everything that life had to offer her.

She was full of spontaneity. This same eagerness for all led to tantrums when her desires were thwarted. Like most children who are the youngest, she had a talent for getting what she wanted from family members. Fortunately her mother and sisters helped to channel Thérèse's energies in more positive directions. Thérèse said, "It was enough for one to say a thing wasn't good and I had no desire to repeat it." She said later that from the age of three she had never refused her God anything.

Even at this early age, Thérèse and Céline used beads to record their daily "practices." Beads were counted both to note their small acts of virtue and equally small imperfections. Thérèse, especially, was unusually sorrowful for actions such as pushing or hitting Céline or tearing a piece of wallpaper. She would immediately run to report her imperfection and with tears beg for forgiveness.

Family Excursions

A favorite Martin family recreation was evening and, especially, Sunday afternoon walks when Mme. Martin could leave her lacemaking and join them. The whole family would enjoy together the delights of nature. Thérèse found great happiness in these walks and wrote later that she still felt "the profound and poetic impressions" that the "fields enameled with cornflowers and all types of wild flowers" had given her. She was in love with the wide open spaces she had experienced earlier in the simple cottage with her nurse, Rose.

Sometimes on these walks, the Martins would meet a poor person. Thérèse was given the duty of pressing some money into the person's hand. This act of generosity gave the little girl great joy. Sometimes, though, the walk would be too long for her, and then her father would lift her into his arms and take her home before the others, in spite of her protests.

One longer trip Thérèse made alone with her mother. They traveled by train to the Visitation Convent in Le Mans. There they visited Sister Marie-Dosithee, Zélie's sister, and Marie and Pauline, who were studying there. Why the train trip brought Thérèse to tears even she could not explain. When they arrived at the convent, she had red eyes and a tear-streaked face. She was soon comforted with a basket of goodies. Thérèse was overjoyed because she would have a gift for Céline when they reached home. Unfortunately, when she took her mother's hand for the return walk to the train, the candies spilled on the

street, and the tears flowed again because she had no gift for her beloved Céline.

Love of Her Parents

As could be expected, Thérèse was devoted to both parents. She wrote later, "I loved Papa and Mama very much and showed my tenderness for them in a thousand ways."

She loved to play a game with her mother. As Thérèse came down the stairs, she would stop on each step and say, "Mama."

If her mother did not answer, Thérèse would remain firmly on the step until she heard, "Yes, my little girl." If Zélie was occupied or forgot to answer immediately, Thérèse remained stationary until she heard her mother's response.

Once Thérèse sweetly announced, "Oh! I would love for you to die, my dear little mother!" Zélie, obviously surprised by the words, questioned her. The little girl's answer was simple: "It's so you go to heaven, since you say we have to die to go there."

At another time Zélie wrote that Thérèse wanted to be always at her side and didn't like to be in the garden unless her mother was there with her. Once she asked her mother if she would go to heaven. Zélie answered with the condition "Yes, if you are good."

Thérèse knew that if she was not good she would go to hell, but she was not worried because if she were in hell, she said, "I know what I'll do. I will fly to you in Heaven, and what will God be able to do to take me away? You will be holding me so tightly in your arms." To Thérèse, this God she knew to be all-powerful would not be able to take her away from her mother's embrace.

Thérèse's father adored her from the moment of her birth. He, of course, loved all his daughters, but a special relationship developed with his youngest. He referred to her as his queen and to himself as king. When he would arrive home, Thérèse would rush to meet her king and position herself on his boot so that she could ride around the house on it.

According to Zélie, Thérèse also prayed for her father that he might die and therefore go to heaven. The relationship between father and daughter would become even stronger after the death of Mme. Martin.

The Loss of a Mother

Zélie had not been well for a number of years and had been unable to nurse her younger children because of a lump in her breast. When the lump became more painful, a doctor was consulted. Zélie learned that it was too late for an operation, and she did not have long to live. Just about this time Zélie's sister, the Visitation nun, was dying of tuberculosis. With her death, Zélie's own health further deteriorated.

Zélie and the three older girls, Marie, Pauline, and Léonie, made a trip to Lourdes in June of 1877, perhaps hoping for a cure. (The younger girls had not been told that their mother would soon die.) Instead of helping Zélie, the trip exhausted her. A cure was not to be. When she returned, she continued her lace business and running her home with Marie's help. Although she must have regretted leaving her beloved husband and five daughters, she was not concerned for their future—except for Léonie, who had a more difficult nature and would, indeed, find it more difficult to get settled. Léonie would finally enter the Visitation Convent. Of Thérèse, her mother said, "...she will be good, you can see the beginnings of it already, she speaks only of God. This little one will manage."

In the two weeks before Zélie's death, Céline and Thérèse were quickly dressed in the morning and sent off to stay with a neighbor for the day. But all were present at Zélie's bedside for the last anointing. Thérèse describes it: "I still see the place where I stood next to Céline. All five of us were in line according to age, and poor Papa was there too, sobbing."

Zélie's death on August 28, 1877, would bring to a close the time Thérèse called the first part of her life. Only later would the full effect of her mother's death be evident. Louise, the nanny, looking at the two youngest remarked, "Poor little ones, you no longer have a mother!"

Hearing this Céline ran to Marie's arms, saying, "You will be my Mama!" Instead of imitating Céline, as she often did, Thérèse rushed to Pauline declaring, "For me, Pauline will be my Mama!"

Reflection

Thérèse, as we have seen, was surrounded by love and gave love in return. The love received and the love given to others molded her character and prepared her for a life dedicated to loving God. We can imitate Thérèse and make ourselves more pleasing to Our Savior by loving those whose lives touch ours: family members, neighbors, and those who enter our lives each day.

St. Thérèse, stir up in our hearts a deeper love of God.

CHAPTER THREE

A NEW HOME AT LES BUISSONNETS

There are things the heart feels
but which the tongue and even the mind cannot express.
The Story of a Soul

Thérèse had wished death for her mother so that she could go to heaven, but the reality of losing her would mark Thérèse in ways that even her father and her sisters could not realize. Of course, it also marked her father, who at fifty-four was alone with five girls to continue raising. He sold the lacemaking business and invested the profits. Between that and what he and Zélie had previously saved, he knew he could be free to spend his time with his girls.

Although Marie, the oldest at seventeen, had learned to manage the household, Louis, with prodding and encouragement from Zélie's brother and sister-in-law, Isidore and Céline Guérin, decided to move closer to the Guérin family in Lisieux. Isidore, a pharmacist, found the Martin family a new home. In

November, just two months after Zélie's death, the family moved to Lisieux.

Although the house, situated on the outskirts of town, was a hundred years old, it was in good condition. It was surrounded by high walls with a flower bed in front of the house and a vegetable garden with trees in the back. The girls named their new home Les Buissonnets, which means little thickets, no doubt for the shrubs and small trees. The garden gate opened to a small uphill walk that M. Martin enjoyed and named "the path to paradise." Close by was a lovely public garden where the Martins would spend many happy hours. In all, it seemed a perfect place for the Martin girls and the reclusive Louis.

Thérèse's reaction was typical of a young child. She wrote, "I did not feel any great disappointment at leaving Alençon: children like change, and I came to Lisieux with pleasure." She would spend the next eleven years of her life in this new environment.

The house had a basement and an attic with two floors between. On the first floor were a kitchen with a large fireplace, a dining room that opened to the front garden, and two other rooms. The second floor was all bedrooms, one for M. Martin and one for the two older girls, Marie and Pauline. Léonie had her own room and the two youngest, Thérèse and Céline, shared a room that looked out on the back garden. The third floor attic had three small rooms and another room M. Martin used as a study for prayer, reading, and writing. This room was a special treasure because the windows looked out on a view that surveyed all of Lisieux, including the bell tower of Saint-Jacques that would become the Martins' parish church.

Thérèse's Deepening Relationship with Her Father

Thérèse tells us that after the death of her mother, her happy disposition completely changed. She says, "I, once so full of life, became timid and retiring, sensitive to an excessive degree. One look was enough to reduce me to tears....I could not bear the company of strangers and found my joy only within the intimacy of the family." But within her family, and especially with her father, she found great happiness. One of their special times together was in their garden. Here Thérèse built little altars in holes or niches in the wall and decorated them with small flowers. Once her decorating work was completed, she would call for her papa to come. Giving him instructions to close his eyes tightly, she would drag him to view her creation. Once permitted to look, he would praise her work, sometimes excessively, but in such a way that would be pleasing to her. At other times she would create in a cup a mixture of sand and twigs from the garden to serve her father tea. He would pretend to drink the concoction with appreciation. She says of her father at this time, that his "very affectionate heart seemed to be enriched now with a truly maternal love."

One of her special joys was when her papa would take her fishing with him. She would sometimes sit with a small pole, but most often she would decorate herself with wild flowers and sit quietly. She says, "Without knowing what it was to meditate, my soul was absorbed in real prayer." But she saw even these occasions tainted with sorrow. When she unpacked the jelly sandwich that Pauline had prepared for her, she found that the jelly had run and the bread seemed stale. To Thérèse this was proof that earth was a place of exile and true happiness would be found only in heaven.

One day their fishing trip was interrupted by a thunderstorm. Thérèse was delighted with the thunder and lightning; she felt it was a sign that God was near. The wild daisies, as tall as Thérèse, were covered with large drops of water that she saw as diamonds. M. Martin, however, was more practical in this instance and scooped up the young Thérèse to carry her and the fishing rods home safely.

In the afternoons Thérèse and her father would frequently go for walks, stopping at different churches for visits to the Blessed Sacrament. During these walks Thérèse would again be given coins to give to the poor that they might meet. Once when Thérèse was just six, the invalid she approached refused her offering, feeling perhaps that he wasn't poor enough. She felt somehow that she had given him pain, and since she had heard that at her first communion God would give her whatever she asked for, she resolved to pray for the man. Five years later at her first communion she remembered her promise and prayed for him.

A Typical Day at Les Buissonnets

In these early days at Les Buissonnets, the household revolved around Thérèse. Soon she was old enough to begin her own lessons with Marie and Pauline. Céline was by now a day student at a school run by the Benedictine sisters. Léonie was a boarder there. Pauline, now her surrogate mother, would awaken her, ask her if she had lifted her heart to God, and then help her to dress. Then Thérèse and Pauline would kneel together to say their morning prayers

After breakfast, the lessons would begin. Marie gave Thérèse instructions in writing and Pauline did all the rest. Thérèse had a good memory and particularly enjoyed lessons in the catechism and in sacred history but remembers crying over grammar lessons. Each day she was given marks for her work. Pauline also gave her points for good behavior. When she had accumulated a number of these, she was given a day free from lessons. Collecting her marks and her points, Thérèse would climb up to the third floor study to show her record to her papa and receive his praise.

The afternoons were free for walks and visits to churches, or fishing with her father, or playing in the garden, with her father ever in attendance. Late in the afternoon the child, called by her father his "crowning glory," but also a "blonde scatterbrain," settled to do her homework. These were happy days for the child Thérèse, as long as she did not have to deal with strangers.

The evenings, particularly Sunday evenings in the winter, were a time of special pleasure. The family would play a game of checkers. After this, Céline and Thérèse would fly to their papa's lap and he would sing or recite poetry for them. Pauline or Marie would read from some instructive book. Finally, all together, the family would go to the second floor and kneel together for evening prayers. Thérèse says of these times that she had only to look at her father to know how the saints prayed.

After prayers, each of the girls, with the oldest first, would approach their father for a kiss goodnight. Since Thérèse was last, she had time to anticipate this special moment. She was still small enough that Pauline would then carry her to the room Thérèse shared with Céline. As Pauline tucked her in, she would invariably ask, "Was I very good today? Will the little angels fly around me?" Pauline always answered, "Yes." She knew that Thérèse feared the dark, and the thoughts of angels would comfort her.

Making Her First Confession

One of the special lessons Pauline gave Thérèse was to prepare her for her first confession. One might wonder what she would have to confess. That she fell into a bucket and had to be rescued by the maid, Victoire? Or that she became so angry she cried when Victoire laughed during a devotion at Thérèse's little May altar? Thérèse remembered being very repentant for this, but not for another occasion when she called Victoire a brat. That time she felt justified.

Pauline had explained that Thérèse would be speaking to God when she confessed her sins. Accepting the instruction literally, Thérèse asked if she should tell the priest that she loved him with all her heart since she was speaking to God.

She was so tiny that she had to stand in the confessional so the priest could see and hear her. The priest advised her to increase her devotion to the Blessed Mother and she promised to do that. After the confession, she wrote that she had experienced the greatest joy of her life.

Visiting with the Guérins

Sometimes on feast days, and almost always after Sunday Mass, the Martins would join the Guérins for a festive meal. Thérèse and Céline would enjoy games with their two cousins, ten-year-old Jeanne, and Marie, who was seven and a half when the Martins first arrived in Lisieux. Often one or more of the Martin girls would stay for the afternoon with the Guérins. Thérèse did not like to stay there alone. She was just a little frightened of her Uncle Isidore with his deep, husky voice. Also he frequently asked her questions that she would answer with only a word or two. She was too frightened and shy to answer more completely.

She looked forward eagerly to her father arriving to take her home. One evening on the walk home she remembered seeing in the sky a special arrangement of stars that to Thérèse resembled the letter *T*. She was delighted and called her father's attention to the display because she felt her name was already written in heaven.

One summer the Martin family took turns joining the Guérins at Trouville, a seaside resort. Thérèse was fascinated by the sea, which spoke to her of the majesty and power of God. It was on this trip that Thérèse was admired by a passerby who commented on her beauty. Before this, she had no idea she was pretty. Her sisters and her father had tried to keep her innocent of vanity. She saw her father shake his head to forestall any further comments, and from this she learned a lesson.

The Vision

Thérèse said of her father, "I cannot say how much I loved Papa; everything in him caused me to admire him." Once when he was working on a ladder, he cautioned Thérèse who was standing below to move lest he should fall from the height and crush her. This only caused her to stand more closely so that if he fell, she would go to heaven with him. Her love for her father was so great that the impact of a vision Thérèse saw about this time in her life was to remain with her forever. She would not fully understand the vision until later when she was in Carmel and able to accept the sad message that was conveyed.

It was early afternoon and Thérèse was at one of the attic windows overlooking the garden. M. Martin was at that time in Alençon on family business. Thérèse saw the figure of a man resembling her father in size, physical appearance, and clothing. The man, however, was stooped and walking slowly. His face appeared to be veiled, but Thérèse was sure it was her father returning from his trip. She called out in delight, "Papa, papa."

Marie, in a nearby room, also had a strange feeling and rushed to Thérèse, explaining that their father was still in Alençon and could not be in the garden. They both went to the garden to check where Thérèse had last seen the figure, but no sign remained.

Only many years later, when Thérèse was recalling these events for her sister Marie, now also a Carmelite, did they both realize that she had indeed seen her father in the suffering that he would endure toward the end of his life. Thérèse's reflection on this was to note the goodness of God. She said, "He parcels out trials only according to the strength he gives us."

Reflection

Thérèse was fortunate in being surrounded by the love and devotion of her sisters and her father. This love would give her strength for the trials that were soon to come. If we, too, have been given great love as a child, we should reach out to others with love. If, on the other hand, we were not as cherished as Thérèse was, it is not a sign that we weren't cherished equally by our heavenly Father. And again our response should be seen in our love for others.

St. Thérèse, help us to love and cherish those who are close to us.

CHAPTER FOUR

THE HARDSHIPS BEGIN

Our steps are made firm by the LORD,…
Though we stumble, we shall not fall…
for the LORD holds us by the hand.
Psalm 37:23–24

Thérèse had been learning at home from Marie and Pauline, but it was now time for her to join Céline as a day boarder at the Benedictine school that Léonie had just left. Also attending were her cousins, Jeanne and Marie. Thérèse said of her school years, "The five years I spent at school were the saddest in my life." Without the presence of Céline, she felt she could never have remained there. Evenings at home, after being picked up either by her father or her uncle, were a joy and a blessing, but the only real relief she found was on the weekends when she said "my heart expanded."

Academic Pluses and Minuses

Because of her home schooling, Thérèse entered the "green class," or the fourth level, with girls who were older than she. Everyone wore the same black uniform with a white collar and a colored sash. The color of the sash indicated the student's level. The girls studied French and English, both of which involved reading and writing, arithmetic and spelling as well. Lessons were also offered in drawing, needlework, piano, violin, mandolin, and deportment.

Thérèse was in a class with slightly older girls, but she was soon at the top of the class in most of the subjects. One can easily imagine that a high achieving, pretty girl, with light brown curls and gray eyes, would incite envy in others, especially since she was younger than the rest.

Reading was a pleasure for Thérèse. She particularly enjoyed tales of chivalry and found delight in the life of Joan of Arc, who was not yet canonized. In most subjects, Thérèse earned honors that she carried home with pride to show her beloved father. But arithmetic and spelling continued to be difficult. Added to these problems, Thérèse heartily disliked Thursday afternoons when she and Céline visited their cousins and were forced to dance quadrilles.

But the worst difficulty for Thérèse was that she was teased excessively, both for her achievements and her appearance. The jealousy of the other girls led her to tears. Unfortunately the tears provided more ammunition for her tormenters. Soon she was labeled a crybaby. When a teacher asked her why she was crying,

she answered, "I'm crying for the sake of crying." She
was not going to turn in her tormentors.

She wanted to make friends, but since she did not
enjoy the same activities that others did, she found it
difficult to enter into their games. She had spent her previous years either playing alone or with Céline, or sometimes in the company of her father. Later she found
pleasure during recess by telling stories to younger girls.
She was even teased for this. The teachers wanted the
girls to be more active, so they were discouraged from
story telling. Twice Thérèse made a friend, but the friend-
ships did not outlast the summer vacation. She wrote,
"When I saw my schoolmate again, my joy was great, but
alas! I got only an indifferent look." She felt the loss
keenly but was not about to beg for another's affection.
Remember that when she was younger, she wouldn't
bend down to pick up a coin when her mother tested her.

Perhaps wishing to make friends, Thérèse was once
caught giving an answer to another child. When
scolded, she burst into tears as usual. She said she cried
not because she had been caught and reprimanded,
but because "I have sinned and have caused another to
sin." Her conscience, as developed by her mother,
Marie, and Pauline, became increasingly sensitive. She
noted, "I really was unbearable because of my too-
great sensitivity."

Pauline Decides to Enter Carmel

Thérèse's school problems were nothing compared
to a new sorrow that was about to devastate her.

Pauline, who was now twenty one, had been thinking about entering the convent. Marie was taking care of the house. Thérèse and Céline were busy at school as day students. Pauline finally felt herself free to pursue her vocation. Her first thought was the Visitation Convent in Le Mans where she had been a boarder in the school and where she had visited her aunt many times. But while at a Mass celebrating the third centenary of the death of St. Teresa of Avila, Pauline recalled a deceased friend of hers who had planned to enter Carmel and take the name Agnès of Jesus. Pauline felt inspired to become a Carmelite instead and to take the name her friend had wanted.

She confided in Marie, who thought she might be too frail for the difficult life of a Carmelite. Pauline assured her that she was quite able. Next she sought the permission and the blessing of her father, her uncle, her confessor, and the mother superior of Carmel, Mother Marie de Gonzague. All were pleased with her decision, although her father must have been both pleased and saddened to lose the girl he called "the Fine Pearl." She would be the first of his five daughters he would return to God.

For some reason, Pauline did not share her decision to enter Carmel with her three younger sisters. During the summer, Thérèse learned she was to lose her second mother when she overheard Pauline and Marie talking about Pauline's coming departure. Thérèse was shattered. She said the news "was like a sword piercing my heart." Again, she realized how transitory happiness in this world can be. This wasn't the simple disappointments of her childhood, like finding her jelly sandwich had become soggy: this was the loss of her idol, the sister who dressed her, taught her, and consoled her. She said, "In an instant I understood what life was; until then I had not imagined it could be so sad, but it appeared to me in its stark reality. I saw that it was only continual suffering and separation. I shed bitter tears."

The next day she told Pauline what she had over-heard. Pauline immediately tried to explain the life of Carmel to the nine year old. Several years before, Pauline and Thérèse had talked about going off to a desert together like hermits. In Thérèse's mind, Pauline was going to a desert and leaving her behind. What brought Thérèse a measure of peace now was the thought that Carmel was the desert, and God was call-ing her to this desert as well. She said of her vocation to Carmel, "I was so sure of this that there wasn't the least doubt in my heart."

It is easy to assume now that Thérèse's response was an attempt to follow her beloved Pauline. But remem-bering the event years later, Thérèse said, "It was not the dream of a child that lets itself be carried away, but the certitude of a divine call. I wanted to go to Carmel, not for Pauline, but *for Jesus alone.*" This thought com-forted her in the midst of her overwhelming sorrow. Later that year, she asked Mother Marie de Gonzague for permission to enter. Mother Marie believed in Thérèse's vocation, but explained that she could not be accepted before she was sixteen.

On a bright sunny day, the second of October in 1882, the Martins and the Guérins attended Mass together. During Mass, Pauline was accepted into

Carmel, and the cloister door closed behind her. Many tears were shed, particularly by Thérèse. The Martins would be able to see Pauline once a week through the grille in the parlor of the monastery. This was, however, no comfort for Thérèse. Since there were so many others who wanted to talk with the new Sister Agnès of Jesus, Thérèse had very little time with her sister. She remarked that these visits were even more painful than the suffering that preceded Pauline's entrance to Carmel.

The next day school began again. This time Thérèse advanced to the "violet" class, which would prepare for first reception of holy communion. For a moment Thérèse was consoled. Then she learned that she would be denied this blessing since she was born two days too late for the then-current ruling on the age for receiving the Eucharist. Her father visited the bishop, seeking a dispensation for his daughter, but his petition was denied. All of these sorrows heaped together on the ten-year-old Thérèse were more than she could bear.

Thérèse's Strange Illness and Cure

Soon after losing Pauline to Carmel and being denied the Eucharist for another year, Thérèse began experiencing migraine headaches and pains in her stomach. She had trouble sleeping and lost her appetite. Despite having a family that apparently catered to her every whim, these minor symptoms were more or less ignored, and her father prepared to take Marie and

Léonie with him to Paris for Holy Week. Thérèse and Céline would stay with the Guérins.

At the Guérins, conversation often focused on Zélie Martin. Recalling the loss of her mother was too much for the already-suffering Thérèse, who burst into tears. She was put to bed with what began as a strange trembling. A doctor was summoned, but he could make no sure diagnosis. The illness continued, and her symptoms increased. Soon Thérèse was suffering from hallucinations, uncontrolled jerking, and seizures of fright. The Martins were summoned from Paris. It was decided that Thérèse was too ill to move, and so Marie stayed with the Guérins to care for her little sister.

During all this, in her lucid moments, Thérèse insisted that she was going to attend Pauline's upcoming reception of the Carmelite habit on April 6. On that morning, Thérèse suffered an unusually severe seizure. Nevertheless, she got up, pronounced herself well, and was permitted to go to Carmel. To all she appeared full of joy and life as she visited her sister, and she insisted she was "perfectly cured."

After the celebration, Thérèse returned to Les Buissonnets, but again had to be put to bed. This time she was delirious. Marie continued to care for her, and her father began to despair that she would ever get well. She only appeared to improve when a weekly letter from Pauline would arrive for her. Sometimes there would be a gift, such as a doll dressed as a Carmelite. Thérèse would read the letter, reread it, and memorize it. Her uncle felt that these reminders of Carmel were not helping but instead were increasing her problems. But the Carmelites were praying for her. Mother Marie

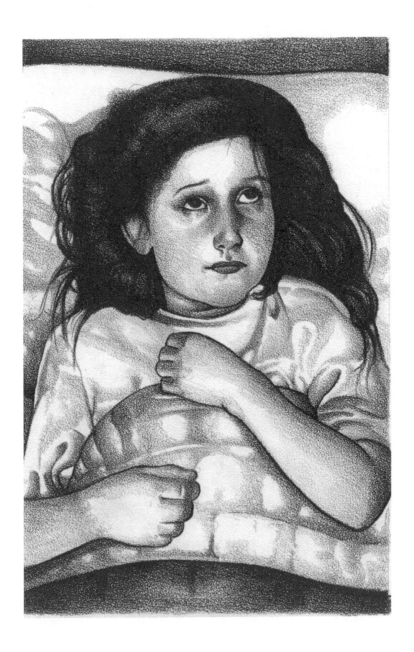

de Gonzague had even written Thérèse, who was already a favorite of hers. And Louis Martin had requested a novena of Masses be said at Our Lady of Victories Church in Paris.

Thérèse was moved to Marie's room. Here the statue of the Blessed Mother, long cherished by the family, was placed near her bed. On the feast of Pentecost, May 13, Léonie was sitting with Thérèse while Marie was busy in the garden. Thérèse, in her delirium, was continually calling, "Mama, Mama." Soon all her sisters were gathered at her bedside praying. Thérèse described what happened then: "All of a sudden the blessed Virgin appeared to me, *beautiful,* more beautiful than anything I had ever seen before. Her face expressed an ineffable goodness and tenderness, but what went right to the depths of my soul was the Blessed Virgin's *ravishing* smile." From this moment Thérèse's pain disappeared, and the next day she was able to resume a normal life. She felt strongly, however, that she should never tell anyone about this miracle lest her happiness disappear. However, she would be unable to keep this promise.

Many have tried to explain Thérèse's illness in psychoanalytic terms, but the best explanation may well be the one that she herself later offered to Pauline: "It certainly came from the devil who was infuriated by your [Pauline's] entrance into Carmel. He wanted to take revenge on me for the wrong our family was to do to him in the future."

Instead of returning to school immediately, Thérèse was given a holiday in Alençon. She returned to the friends of her childhood after more than six years away. There she was "entertained, coddled, admired." It was a time of happiness for the child of ten and a half, who had lost "two mothers" in six years. The attention poured on her might have seemed preferable to the desert of Carmel. Thérèse, however, saw these as Jesus offering her an opportunity to choose to follow him freely, having tasted and turned away from the world's pleasures.

A priest who met her at this time said, "What struck me strongly about this child was her simplicity, her ingenuity, and her innocence....But what is particularly remarkable in a child of that age is that she related nothing to herself and forgot herself entirely, using none of her advantages to her benefit."

Reflection

We may not be favored with a special smile from the Blessed Virgin to heal us from physical or mental suffering. But if we take our sufferings, large and small, and place them in her hands, if it is for our spiritual well-being, we will be healed. If healing doesn't come, we can ask the Holy Spirit for strength to endure the suffering. We have much to learn from Thérèse, who was only ten years old when these truths were apparent to her.

St. Thérèse, teach us to take our burdens to Our Lady who will surely smile on us whether we see the smile or not.

CHAPTER FIVE

TORMENTS AND CONSOLATIONS

Oh God, from my youth you have taught me,
and I still proclaim your wondrous deeds.

Psalm 71:17

When Thérèse returned to school in October of 1883, she was now considered old enough to prepare for her first holy communion. She was an eager student, but she was haunted by two interior trials, which had begun before the vacation. First, though she had promised herself not to tell anyone of the remarkable vision of Our Lady and her cure, she had told Marie, then Marie had told the Carmelites. Thérèse's joy became a source of suffering as she was questioned about the vision. She was horrified that she had broken her promise. Even more severe was the thought that was to burden her for five years. Had she brought her illness on herself, and then had she perhaps lied about the vision? She tried to talk to Marie and her confessor about this, but nothing would put her mind at rest.

First Holy Communion

Without being aware of it, Thérèse had long been practicing mental prayer. While fishing with her father as a youngster, she would think of the rewards of eternity. In later years, she would find times and places where she could be alone and let thoughts of her loving Lord comfort her, particularly when she was suffering at school. When the world outside her family seemed to treat her harshly, she took refuge in talking to her One True Friend. This interior prayer was a great preparation for her first communion. But from October to May, she received other instructions as well.

In a booklet of notes that Thérèse kept at this time, she wrote the titles of various instructions given by the priest: Hell, Death, Sacrilegious Communion, The Last Judgment. These are frightening topics for children, but they were typical of the preparation given at the time. And even though Thérèse's later message to the world was seemingly not shaped by these instructions, they no doubt contributed to another trial she would soon suffer.

Both Pauline and Marie helped Thérèse with this important preparation. Pauline had sent from Carmel a little book bound in blue velvet that she had made for her little sister. It described daily sacrifices to be made for Jesus. Thérèse recorded that from March to May she made 1,949 sacrifices and had repeated the prayers or invocations suggested by Pauline 2,773 times. (That's an average of thirty-two sacrifices and forty-six short prayers a day.) Marie had given her a booklet titled "Renunciation"—certainly not joyful reading, but instruction taken to heart by Thérèse. Marie also taught her that the way to be holy was to be faithful in little things. This is a lesson Thérèse learned well. She was convinced that the worst sinners could be brought to repentance just by listening to Marie.

Most of the girls at the Abbey would make a month-long retreat at the school. Because of Thérèse's delicate condition, her retreat was shortened to three days in May. Even in the short retreat she was again subjected to ridicule because she was so used to being cared for by Marie or Pauline. Though eleven, she wasn't accustomed to washing and dressing herself and found this a new difficulty. The simple act of brushing and preparing her own hair in the morning was something she had never before done for herself.

May 8, 1884, however, dawned a joyful day. Thérèse received Jesus in the Eucharist, saying, "I love you; I give myself to you forever." She felt she had received "a kiss of love" from her Lord. The emotion of this meeting brought her to tears, but they were tears of joy. In the evening her joy increased when she went to Carmel to celebrate with Pauline. Pauline had that day made her profession as a Carmelite. She was dressed in white like Thérèse and wore a crown of roses.

Thérèse could hardly wait for her next opportunity to receive communion. At that time, permission from a confessor was needed in order to receive, and such permission was not given very often. On May 22, Ascension Thursday, she was permitted to receive for the second time. At this time she thought of the words of St. Paul: "Yet, I live, no longer I, but Christ lives in me." In this union that she felt so strongly, she recognized and welcomed the crosses that she knew awaited her. She felt "a great desire to suffer."

Another two-day retreat soon followed, to prepare for the sacrament of confirmation three weeks later on June 14. When Thérèse received this sacrament, she felt the Holy Spirit had given her the strength to suffer. She was eleven years old.

Summer Holiday

After her first communion, Thérèse asked her father for a dog. She was given a white spaniel she named Tom. She delighted in the joyful companionship of her little dog. A bout of whooping cough in July weakened her, so her father rented a farmhouse in the country. Here Marie, Léonie, Céline, Thérèse, and Tom enjoyed the pleasures of country living. Thérèse's face was soon shining with health and happiness. She enjoyed the farm's ponds, the odors of hay and honeysuckle, the stream and the woods near the farm. While on holiday she made drawings and paintings of her surroundings. These were remarkably good for a child of her age.

Soon it was time to return to school. This year Céline would complete her studies, and her cousin Marie would be taken from school because of sickness. Thérèse would be without family and was consequently terribly unhappy. To add to her difficulties, she endured an overly sensitive conscience, and a retreat brought on a terrible affliction.

Scruples

It was almost inevitable that one as sensitive as Thérèse would be subject to scruples. Thérèse called it "a terrible sickness," and it is. It is a spiritual disease that causes one to be always fearful of the least suggestion of sin. Even at three, Thérèse would run to her mother to confess her minor failings. Her distress over breaking her promise to not tell of the visit from Our Lady is another example. Thérèse said, "All my most simple thoughts and actions became the cause of trouble for me." The fear of offending God and her inability to find peace through confession were undoubtedly worsened by the theology of the time, which stressed hell and damnation. She said, "One would have to pass through this martyrdom to understand it well, and for me to express what I suffered for a year and a half would be impossible."

She experienced some relief when she burdened Marie with her supposed sins. Thérèse acknowledged that she must have been an awful pest to Marie. To try to help her overcome this prolonged trial, Marie would tell her what to confess, in an attempt to assure her that most of her sins were not really sins. Despite Marie's help, suffering these scruples and being alone at school again brought on a recurrence of Thérèse's terrible headaches.

While in school, she was received into the Association of the Holy Angels, which gave her pleasure since she had a particular devotion to her guardian angel. She had also hoped to be received into the sodality of the Children of Mary, but as her headaches increased, it was decided that she should leave the school, and attendance at school was necessary for membership. No doubt her aunt and uncle approved of her leaving school since they thought her to be "a little dunce, good and sweet, with right judgment, yes, but incapable and clumsy."

Because all her sisters had been sodality members, Thérèse asked for special permission to belong. She feared she would not be as close to Our Lady as her sisters were. But being a member of the sodality was to be another cause of pain. In order to be accepted in the sodality, she was required to return to school for several hours a week. Thérèse felt alone there. She says, "No one paid any attention to me." She, however, made good use of her time by spending hours before the Blessed Sacrament.

A New Way of Life

And so began a strange new learning experience for Thérèse. Several times a week she went to the home of Mme. Papinau for her lessons. Mme. Papinau, who was fifty years old, lived with her mother and her cat. Often the lessons were interrupted by visitors: priests, ladies, and young girls who discussed the gossip of Lisieux. Although Thérèse tried to keep her head buried in her textbook, she could not help but overhear. Sometimes what she overheard was a question like, "Who is that pretty young girl?" Thérèse would blush and be haunted by the sin of vanity, which she felt such comments aroused.

At home, she took over one of the attic rooms for her own study. She took great pleasure in decorating the room, which she called a "bazaar," probably because of the many odds and ends she assembled there. Her love of nature expressed itself with a large aviary full of birds, an aquarium with goldfish, and a window box with rare plants. Of course, there was a picture of her beloved Pauline, as well as statues of saints and the Blessed Mother. Here Thérèse could study, prepare her lessons, read, meditate, and pray.

In June, her aunt and uncle invited her to another vacation in the country at the Chalet des Lilas. Although Thérèse usually flourished in the country, this time she was lonely. No one from Les Buissonnets was there with her. Her aunt decided to send her home, but not before Thérèse had done another drawing of the vacation spot. As soon as she returned home, she was again well. Thérèse decided she had been homesick.

Reflection

Thérèse's bout with scruples is an interior trial that most of us will not suffer. But the sensitivity of her conscience is something we might want to strive for. She says that from the age of three she never knowingly offended God. If we can make God more central to our daily living, we will be more aware of the things in our nature that are offensive to him.

St. Thérèse, help us to form a conscience pleasing to God.

CHAPTER SIX

THE NIGHT OF CONVERSION

O LORD my God, I cried to you for help,
and you have healed me.
Psalm 30:2

At thirteen, Thérèse was still very much a child, loved and cared for by her family, but having difficulty handling any situation that forced her to deal with anyone who was not a member of her immediate household. She was not even comfortable vacationing with her aunt and uncle unless one of her sisters was present. Tremendous emotional growth would be needed to transform this sheltered, overly sensitive girl into the young woman who would be canonized and declared a Doctor of the Church. The events of the next year would culminate in this needed transformation.

Marie Plans to Enter Carmel

In October of 1886, Thérèse learned that Marie, who was now twenty six and her confidante and support, had decided to join Pauline in Carmel. Thérèse was devastated. She was still suffering from scruples. Now she would have no one to give her relief and peace from this affliction. She admitted she made a pest of herself, often knocking on Marie's door for a kiss and some assurance. Thérèse said she was trying to build up a store of affection for when Marie would be gone. M. Martin was also saddened by his eldest's coming departure. This daughter, whom he called "the diamond," had been his right hand in raising the younger girls for nine years since the death of their mother. Nevertheless, he and her uncle were pleased to support her decision.

As a diversion, he took the family for one more trip to Alençon to visit the grave of the girls' mother. It would be the last time Marie would have that opportunity since once in Carmel, she would never leave. As happened so often, Thérèse dissolved in tears, not so much for the loss of her mother as because she had forgotten to bring the bouquet of cornflowers that she had picked for the grave.

While they were at Alençon, Léonie shocked them all. She had gone to the convent of the Poor Clares for a visit and asked to be immediately accepted as a postulant in the Order. She had discussed her sudden decision with no one in her family, and they were justifiably upset. Marie had assumed that Léonie would be looking after the two younger girls, Céline and Thérèse. Their Uncle Guérin, who expected to be consulted in these matters, predicted that Léonie would soon be returning to Lisieux.

Léonie's bombshell did not, however, interfere with Marie's plans to enter Carmel. Their father would not allow that to happen. So, on the feast of St. Teresa of Avila, October 15, Marie joined Pauline, Sister Agnès of Jesus, in the Lisieux Carmel and took the name Sister Marie of the Sacred Heart.

Scruples Are Cured

The convent's double grille had not been a place of happiness for Thérèse and she would continue to find it frustrating. She had hated the limitations the grille put on her conversations with Pauline. There was never enough time, and too many people were also visiting. Now the grille would also prevent her from confiding her troubles to Marie.

She had to find some relief from the interior pain that scruples inflicted. In her distress, she turned to heaven and prayed to the four brothers and sisters who had been born and died before her birth. The family had revered these lost children as saints, so Thérèse felt confident that they would help her. She explained to them her position as youngest and "most loved" child, one who had been "showered with my sisters' tender care." She was sure that, although in heaven, they had not forgotten her and begged them to obtain for her the peace of mind and heart that she so badly needed. Her prayers were soon answered. She says, "Peace poured into my soul," and she knew she was loved in heaven as she was on earth. The extremes of her scruples disappeared, but she still remained overly emotional.

Sensitivity and Tears Continue

When Thérèse visited Marie in the parlor on Thursdays, she would cry. When Marie admonished her for this, Thérèse "cried for having cried." She said, "I was really unbearable because of my extreme touchiness" and described herself as "the most unhappy creature of the world."

At home at Les Buissonnets, Céline was now in charge of the bedroom they shared. Thérèse was still shielded from housework of any kind. When she offered to help make her bed, for instance, her efforts were so disastrous that Céline would have to remake it. And so Thérèse wept. Further, she was upset that Céline did not at least commend her for her efforts. How could this young weepy girl, almost fourteen, ever withstand the rigors of life in Carmel? And yet she was still determined to enter, not to join her sisters, but because she felt that Jesus was calling her there.

The Miracle of Christmas

Christmas of 1886 was not a happy time at Les Buissonnets. As her uncle had predicted, Léonie returned home from the Poor Clares. As a postulant, her hair had been cut short. She had to wear a mantilla to hide her haircut, and although she was twenty-three, her face was seriously broken out. She was humiliated and ashamed by the failure of her vocation. Céline and Thérèse did what they could to comfort her, but it was a sad time for them all.

On Christmas eve, M. Martin and his three daughters went to the cathedral for midnight Mass. Thérèse, and no doubt the others, received holy communion. It was an evening filled with grace for the family, but more was to come. Before Mass, Thérèse had placed her shoes beside the fireplace at home to be filled with gifts, the tradition for little children in France. Céline, who still treated her like a child, had dutifully filled the shoes with small gifts. In the past, M. Martin always seemed to share in Thérèse's joy as she exclaimed over each tiny gift. But that night was different. Once they arrived home, Thérèse hurried upstairs to remove her hat. At that instant, she overheard her beloved father exclaim, "Well, fortunately, this will be the last year for this!"

Predictably Thérèse responded with tears. Céline, who had followed her, begged her not to go downstairs immediately, certainly not while still crying. Suddenly, Thérèse was transformed, or, as she says, "converted." She dried her tears and went downstairs to open her gifts with a smile. She pretended joy, crushing out the humiliation and hurt of her dear father's words. She said that after this she was seldom able to cry, and certainly not the tears caused by her own hypersensitivity.

Thérèse understood that she had all at once outgrown the character that had developed years before at her mother's death. What she had not been able to do by herself had been accomplished for her in a single moment, and in that moment she matured. Earlier, she had been cured of her strange sickness by a smile from the Blessed Mother. She had then been cured of her dreadful scruples by prayers to her brothers and sisters in heaven. Now she had been cured of her horrible sensitivity. God worked, she said, "a little miracle to make me *grow up* in an instant." Whether or not we choose to call these three events miracles, the youngest Martin girl would become a new person, able to face the world alone and to struggle with authorities to gain early entrance into the Carmelite Order.

Years later she described the events of this Christmas miracle to a priest: "On that blessed night...Jesus, who saw fit to make Himself a child out of love for me, saw fit to have me come forth from the swaddling clothes and imperfections of childhood. He transformed me in such a way that I no longer recognized myself....The Lord clothed me in His divine strength."

Reflection

Thérèse endured many sufferings early in her life, many caused primarily by the loss of her beloved mother, and then later the loss of her second mother, Pauline. But she was also favored with many graces or miracles. It is important to note that the graces did not come easily, and not before years of suffering for a little girl. We can learn from this that if we remain constant in prayer, asking for the graces we need, we will eventually be blessed in God's own time.

St. Thérèse, help us to wait patiently in prayer
for the time of his Grace.

CHAPTER SEVEN

On the Road to Carmel

Let the little children come to me; do not stop them;
for it is to such as these that the kingdom of God belongs.
Mark 10:14

Thérèse called her Christmas miracle a *night of light,* and says it marked the third period of her life, "the most beautiful and the most filled with graces from heaven." She had long enjoyed and treasured the little book *Imitation of Christ,* and used its wisdom to guide her spiritual growth, but in this period she would find new inspirations for spiritual growth.

Growing Mentally, Morally, and Physically

The first few months of 1887 passed peacefully for Thérèse, who was now fourteen. She continued her education with Mme. Papinau. She felt a tremendous desire to learn, not something usually aspired to by young ladies of the time. She asked her father for advice on books of history to read and talked to her uncle, the pharmacist, for suggestions on science books. She continued to study and pray in her attic retreat. From January to May, she took art lessons from Céline, working with still life, portraits, and country scenes. She would have liked to study with the same teacher as Céline, but she recognized that Céline's talent was clearly superior. The relationship of the two sisters, who had always been close, deepened as Thérèse developed emotional, mental, and physical maturity.

During this time Thérèse wrote in her journal, "If my dreams come true, one day I will go and live in the country. When I think about my plan I am carried away in spirit to a delightful sunlit little house, where all my rooms look out on the sea." The little house would be close to a church so that she could attend Mass every day. (At this time, Thérèse had been given permission by her confessor to receive communion four or five times a week.) She would spend her days visiting the poor and the sick, carrying food and medicine. And she would have a few animals for company—a donkey, a cow, some sheep, and some chickens.

A formative influence on the still-impressionable Thérèse was a book she begged her father for permission to read. The Carmelites had lent him *The End of the Present World and the Mysteries of the Future Life.* She copied pages of the book that moved her deeply, particularly the pages on perfect love. She later declared this reading to be "one of the greatest graces in my life." Not only did she find this study inspiring, but also sharing with Céline her thoughts and ideas from her reading was a further grace. Often they would talk until midnight, gazing out at the stars and moon from the little attic room. They were not seeking a worldly lover as girls their age often are, but rather Jesus whom, Thérèse said, they found under a "light and transparent veil."

The graces that flooded her soul at this time allowed her to make daily sacrifices more easily without letting the pain of the sacrifice show in her face. She said, "Immediate renunciation became easy for me." Her love for God had increased so much that it was difficult for her to find a way to express this love. Because there was no one in hell to praise him, she suggested that she would go the depths of hell if that would please him. After making this offering, she said, "When we love, we experience the desire to say a thousand foolish things."

All this time, Thérèse had been returning to school for the required hours so that she could be accepted in the sodality of the children of Mary. Finally, her wish was fulfilled, and she became a member. She dedicated herself to Our Lady, professing her desire to belong to Mary without reserve and to imitate her virtues, especially purity, obedience, and charity.

Surmounting Family Obstacles

One of the things Thérèse had discussed with Céline in their late-night talks was her desire to enter Carmel as soon as possible. Céline, who also wished to enter Carmel, was the older and should have entered first. However, she was more than willing to step aside and support Thérèse through the trials that would come as she sought permission for early entrance.

On the feast of Pentecost, May 1887, while in their garden, Thérèse approached her beloved father for his permission. Although he felt she was young to be making this decision, he was soon convinced that her desire was God's will. He said nothing to deter her resolve and seemed to realize, in his sorrow at losing her, that God was honoring him. He promised to help her deal with the permissions that would be needed to allow one so young to enter the difficult life of Carmel. Then he picked a little white flower that was growing in the stone wall surrounding the garden to present to Thérèse. She pressed the flower in her *Imitation of Christ* in the chapter titled "That You Must Love Jesus Above All Things." This simple white flower, growing in the crevice of a garden rock, was uprooted as Thérèse would be uprooted from the home she loved. The flower became for her a symbol of herself, and she referred to herself as a "Little Flower." She felt that God was saying with this sign that he would soon "break the bonds of His little flower."

Meanwhile, her two sisters in Carmel were divided in their support. Pauline was at first eager to see Thérèse overcome all obstacles to entering. But Marie, who had now been in Carmel about a year, felt that the life was too difficult for someone as young as Thérèse.

Thérèse also had to ask her uncle for his permission, but she did not approach him until October. He was opposed to her entering Carmel for at least three more years, till she was seventeen. Thérèse left his house in sorrow. Four days later, he summoned her back to his

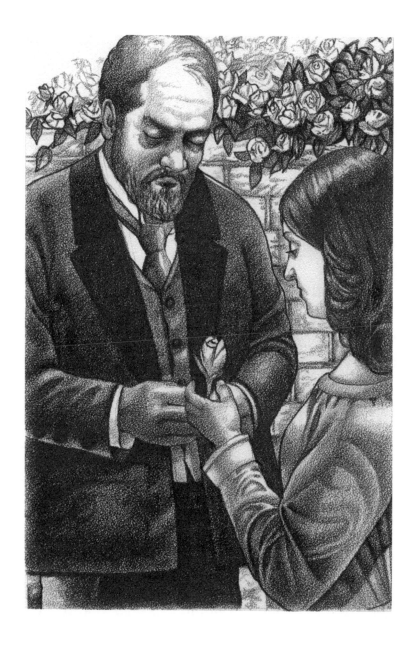

study to announce that he had prayed for a change of heart. The change had come, and he told her that she was *"a little flower God wanted to gather."* He would no longer oppose her entering Carmel. Thérèse was overjoyed.

When she relayed her happiness to Pauline, she was dismayed to learn that the priest responsible for the nuns at the Lisieux Carmel would not give his consent for Thérèse to enter until she was twenty-one. This would be the beginning of many more obstacles to be overcome.

Her "First Child"

During the summer, looking at a picture of Jesus on the cross while at Mass, Thérèse felt a need to collect his sacred drops of blood so she could apply it to the needs of souls. She knew that her vocation, as she would later describe it, was "to love Jesus and to make Him loved."

She would soon find a way to test her vocation of winning souls for Jesus in the person of Henri Pranzini, who had brutally murdered three women. All of France was shocked at the crime. Pranzini was swiftly tried and convicted, although he protested his innocence throughout the trial in spite of solid evidence against him.

Thérèse was not allowed to read the newspaper at home, but she learned of the case, perhaps overhearing someone discuss it. She began to increase her prayers and sacrifices and to have Masses said that Pranzini, who was unrepentant, would be saved. She begged

God to show mercy to him and to give her some sign of Pranzini's repentance. On September 1, after refusing all offers of help from the chaplain, Pranzini went to his execution. At the last minute, he called for a crucifix and kissed it. Learning of this, Thérèse cried tears of joy. Not only had her Lord pardoned Pranzini, but her personal vocation had been confirmed. She felt that the convicted murderer was just the first of the "children" she would save. She acknowledged, "God has no need for anyone to carry out His work, I know" but "Jesus wills to be helped."

More Obstacles to Be Overcome

Thérèse, this shy and timid teenager, had determined that she would enter Carmel on Christmas day of 1887, just days before her fifteenth birthday. Since the priest at Carmel had refused her permission until she was twenty-one, she was determined to overcome this barrier. A first step would be a visit in October to the Bishop of Bayeux and Lisieux. She was frightened at the prospect of seeing the bishop, but she put up her hair in order to appear older. The interview was considerably delayed, which allowed more time for nervousness as well as extra time for prayer. It was also raining, which Thérèse took for a bad omen. When the Vicar General, Father Révérony, finally brought Thérèse and her father to the bishop, he admonished her not to cry before the bishop, but she did. And although the bishop was seemingly charmed by

Thérèse, he could only promise that he would give an answer on the coming trip to Italy.

The trip to Italy was a grand pilgrimage and Louis Martin, Thérèse, and Céline had planned to be part of the group. The Martins left early for Paris, the gathering place for the tour. M. Martin wanted to show the sights of Paris to his two daughters. Thérèse was not impressed. She wrote to Marie and Pauline, "The beautiful things of Paris do not at all captivate my heart." Her heart was set only on going to Italy to ask the pope himself for permission to enter Carmel.

On November 6, 197 pilgrims gathered to travel to celebrate Pope Leo XIII's fiftieth anniversary as a priest. The pilgrims were a mixed group: seventy-five priests, French royalty like counts and viscounts, and "commoners" like the Martins. Céline and Thérèse were the youngest on the trip. Surprisingly, Thérèse was not intimidated by the group and was able to converse happily with them. She said, "I felt as if I had always lived in this world." Father Révérony was also on the pilgrimage and had apparently decided to watch Thérèse carefully. After her tears with the bishop, he was not sure what to expect from her.

The tour traveled through Switzerland, and Thérèse was enchanted with the snowcapped mountains and the waterfalls. She raced from one side of the railroad car to the other so that she would not miss any of the beauty. The first stop in Italy was in Milan, then on to Venice, Padua, and Bologna. She found Venice "sad," but loved Padua and developed a devotion to St. Anthony there. As the youngest, the Martin girls were the most adventurous of the tourists, not wishing to miss anything. Finally the tour reached Rome.

One of the first visits was to the Coliseum. Here Thérèse, in spite of the barriers erected to keep visitors out of the center, grabbed Céline and raced to kneel in the dirt and to kiss the soil that the early martyrs' blood had touched. As she knelt there and prayed, she felt she had been given the grace to be a martyr herself. At every stop on the tour, the two sisters explored everything, determined not to miss anything and to savor all.

Each night the pilgrims stayed in luxurious hotels eating wonderful meals. Here Thérèse was able to observe the priests on the tour and learned to her surprise that priests, too, are human and subject to many of the weaknesses of other human beings. She knew that Carmelite sisters pray especially for priests. Now she commented, "If the most saintly have great need of prayers, what is to be said of those who are lukewarm?" And she vowed to pray always for priests.

Finally the great day arrived. The pilgrims attended Mass said by the Holy Father and then prepared for their visit with him. The women dressed in black with a black mantilla covering their head. Thérèse was filled with trepidation, but knew that all of Carmel was praying for her to be able to express her desire to Pope Leo XIII. If he would give her permission, all the other obstacles would melt away. The pilgrims were lined up, women first, then priests, and finally the lay men. Each would kneel before the pope, then kiss his hand and his slipper. At first, Leo spoke a word of blessing to each pilgrim, but he was seventy-seven and tired easily. Father Révérony, who presented each pilgrim, insisted that each was to remain silent so as not to further tire His Holiness. Thérèse did not know what to do. Disobey? She felt this was her last chance. Céline, who was immediately behind her, whispered, "Speak."

As Thérèse knelt, she kissed the pope's slipper, but instead of kissing his hand, she clasped her hands on his knees and said, "Most Holy Father, I have a great favor to ask you!" He lowered his head to her and she continued, "Holy Father, in honor of your Jubilee, permit me to enter Carmel at the age of fifteen!"

His Holiness did not really understand and turned to Father Révérony, who was standing by his side and was most displeased. The Vicar General responded, "This is a child who wants to enter Carmel at the age of fifteen. The superiors are considering the matter at the moment."

The Holy Father turned back to Thérèse and instructed her to do whatever the superiors would tell her. Desperately she made a final plea, "If you say yes, everybody will agree."

He responded, "Go...go...*You will enter if God wills it.*"

She would have entreated him further, but two guards and Father Révérony lifted her to her feet and dragged her away, but not before the Holy Father placed his hands on her lips and gave her a blessing.

Thérèse was devastated. This had been her last hope. But she remembered that for some time she had offered herself to Jesus as his little ball. She was a toy to play with, throw away, and treat as a very young child treats a toy. She recognized that he had taken her at her word.

On the next day the tour left for Naples and Pompeii, but M. Martin remained in Rome. He took this opportunity to talk to Father Révérony. He was able to convince the Vicar General of the validity of Thérèse's vocation. For the rest of the trip, Father Révérony was solicitous of Thérèse and promised to do all that he could to assure her early entrance to Carmel. Meanwhile, the tour visited Assisi, Florence, Pisa, and Genoa before returning to France on December 3. The Martins were delighted to return to Les Buissonnets. Although Thérèse was saddened, she was still hoping that Christmas day would find her in Carmel.

Reflection

Thérèse had faced many obstacles in her desire to enter Carmel at fifteen, but she met them all with a determined tenacity. She had experienced the wonders of travel in luxury, and although she enjoyed it, the trip only strengthened her longing to be united with her Savior in the strict enclosure of Carmel. For the moment, she was his plaything, his little ball, for him to use as he wished.

St. Thérèse, gain for us your determination,
so that we can overcome obstacles to a more perfect
service of Our Lord.

CHAPTER EIGHT

THE GOAL IS REALIZED

*Whoever becomes humble like this child
is the greatest in the kingdom of heaven.*
Matthew 18:4

Jesus was not in the least finished playing with his little ball. The next few weeks were exceedingly difficult. Having been assured that Father Révérony was going to intercede for her, Thérèse waited daily for some word. Pauline suggested that she write to the bishop to remind him of his promise to give her word in Italy. Her uncle didn't like her letter because he felt it was too "simple." Meanwhile, word came from Pauline to wait a few days, so she did. After the letter was mailed, her father accompanied her to the post office each day after Mass because young ladies at this time did not appear on the streets alone. Each day was a disappointment, and it was getting closer to Christmas day, when she had hoped to be in Carmel.

Another Unexpected Delay

Thérèse reasoned that God "works no miracles *before having tried [one's] faith.*" And her faith was certainly tried. For Christmas, Céline gave her a tiny boat carrying the Child Jesus who had a ball by his side. Céline had named the boat "Abandonment." Thérèse vowed to try to surrender and overcome her frustration at waiting. Later, on Christmas Day at Carmel, the grille was opened to reveal "a radiant little Jesus holding a ball in His hand." Thérèse's name was inscribed on the ball.

Finally, on New Year's day, Mother Marie de Gonzague sent a letter telling Thérèse that the bishop's letter had arrived on December 28, the Feast of the Holy Innocents. Thérèse had not been informed earlier because, of all things, Pauline, who had been a firm supporter throughout all of the difficulties of gaining permission for an early entrance, had advised that Thérèse should wait until after Lent. Pauline, Sister Agnès of Jesus, was afraid the rigors of Lent in Carmel would be too much for her.

Now Thérèse was faced with three more months of waiting. The best thing would be to take things easy and allow herself some small pleasures before her departure from her beloved father and sisters. Instead, Thérèse vowed to practice even more penances than before. However, she characterized these as mere nothings compared to the penances practiced by the saints, or even, she admitted, by Céline. She vowed instead to hold back replies and to do little things for others without expecting any thanks. Such little acts— and she had many of them—helped her to get through the three months as she prepared to become "the fiancée of Jesus."

Meanwhile, Léonie, who had tried earlier to join the Poor Clares, had entered the Visitation Convent in Caen in July. (She was in the convent there when Céline and Thérèse went with their father on the grand trip to Rome.) Now, in January, she had returned home again, depressed with her second failure. She spoke to Thérèse of the difficulties of religious life and warned her to reflect seriously about her decision to enter, especially as young as she was. Thérèse, however, assured Léonie that she had no illusions about the difficulties she would be facing.

Carmel at Last

Thérèse finally learned that April 9, 1888, would be her entrance day. It was the feast of the Annunciation, which had been transferred that year because of Lent. The evening before, the Martins and the Guérins had gathered for a last meal together. The meal of fine food, served on delicate china resting on a soft linen tablecloth, was the last Thérèse would see of such luxury. There were tears, tender words, and embraces. Thérèse felt deeply the pain of saying goodbye to her sisters and to her beloved father, as well as to Les Buissonnets where she had spent ten years of her life.

The next morning all attended Mass at the Carmel chapel. There the sanctuary is divided crossways by a grille with the nuns on one side and the lay people on the other. At communion Thérèse heard crying from the others, but she could not cry. She could only rejoice that the trial of waiting was over. After Mass, Louis Martin accompanied her to the door of the enclosure. There she knelt before her father for his blessing as he presented his youngest to the Lord.

Once the door had closed behind her, Thérèse was led to the choir where she met the twenty-six sisters who would be her daily companions until her death. She knelt before Mother Geneviève of St. Theresa, who had founded the Lisieux convent, and she felt she was in the presence of a saint. Then Mother Marie de Gonzague showed Thérèse the rest of the convent: the oratory, where the nuns prayed when not in the chapel; the kitchen; the refectory, where the nuns ate; the one heated room for recreation; the cloisters; and the garden. Finally, Thérèse was shown her cell on the second floor. The room contained a bed with a straw mattress, a small stool, an oil lamp, and an hourglass. A "cell bench" that had a portable desk completed the furnishings. A plain wooden cross hung on the white wall. At Les Buissonnets, Thérèse had loved gazing from her attic window. Her cell had a window, but it offered only a view of the slate roof of another part of the convent. Her sister Marie had described the convent as small and poor, but Thérèse was thrilled with it all, and said, "No cloud darkened my blue heaven."

The next morning Thérèse, at the age of fifteen, began the normal daily schedule of a Carmelite. She rose at 4:45 in the morning. As a postulant, she dressed in a blue dress and black cape and wore a small cap to hold back her hair. The day began with prayers followed by Mass. In all, Carmelites spent six hours a day in prayer.

When it wasn't a time of fasting, there were three meals but never any meat, unless someone was ill. Five hours were given to manual labor such as cleaning, cooking, gardening, making hosts, sewing, washing—not the kind of work that Thérèse had excelled at before. Seven hours were allowed for sleep in winter.

Thérèse planned to continue her small daily practices of self-denial and self- discipline. Although she had had no illusions about life in the convent, she found there new hardships to be suffered for love. The simple convent food, consisting of meatless soups, vegetables, and bread, was difficult for Thérèse to tolerate, and she frequently had a stomachache.

Living with twenty-six different personalities—many of whom lacked her education, culture, and intelligence—provided daily opportunities for penance. The sisters were united in their goals of striving for perfection, saving souls, interceding for humanity, and praying for priests. That, however, did not mean that the differences in their temperaments and characters would not cause minor frictions and misunderstandings. This would be difficult for anyone to adjust to, but most certainly for a girl of fifteen.

One of the most painful adjustments Thérèse had to make was no longer being the favored child at Les Buissonnets, the one who had been cared for by all. Even though she was united with Pauline and Marie, her sisters could show her no special attention. Further, Mother Marie de Gonzague, who had been a dear mother to her when she was on the outside of the grille, could now show her no particular favor either. She was, after all, mother to all in the convent.

Life as a Postulant

An important part of Thérèse's early days in Carmel was spent with Sister Marie of the Angels, the novice mistress. Although sometimes naïve and frequently distracted, Sister Marie was excellent in explaining the Rule, Constitutions, and customs of the Order to Thérèse and the other three in the novitiate, one of whom was Thérèse's sister, Marie. They learned from her how to eat, how to walk slowly, and how to keep their eyes lowered. The novice mistress found in Thérèse a docile student, but not one very adept at mending, sweeping, and gardening, all things she had not had to do at home.

But if the novice mistress found no fault with Thérèse, others did. Perhaps to help the young girl grow spiritually, Mother Marie humiliated her on almost every encounter. This caused Thérèse great pain, especially because she had once felt so loved by her. Other sisters thought Thérèse to be a "grand lady," not one who would be of much use to the community.

Thérèse spent her little free time writing letters. She wrote to her father, who missed her greatly. She wrote to Céline, who wished to be with her in Carmel. She even wrote to Pauline and Marie while they were away on private retreats. For example, a few days before Marie was to make profession of her perpetual vows, Thérèse wrote to ask for her prayers: "I feel like you are an angel....You who are an eagle destined to soar on the heights and stare at the sun, pray for the little reed, so weak."

May brought much happiness to Carmel and to Thérèse. It was the fiftieth anniversary of the founding of this particular convent, which meant celebrations. Marie would make her profession and receive her black veil. Further, Father Pichon, who had directed both Pauline and Marie on their way to Carmel, was back from Canada.

Thérèse took advantage of his presence to make a general confession, one that reviews all the sins of one's life. This confession brought her great peace. She said that afterwards Father Pichon said, "In the presence of the good Lord, of the Holy Virgin, and of all the saints, I declare that never have you committed a single mortal sin." Great relief flooded her soul. The pain of scruples was over. Then he added, "Thank the good Lord for what He has done for you, for if He abandoned you, instead of being a little angel, you would become a little demon." Thérèse agreed and said, "I felt how weak and imperfect I was, but gratitude filled my soul."

Louis Martin Is Ill

Also in May, M. Martin talked to his three daughters in Carmel about a visit he had made to Alençon to visit Zélie's grave. When he stopped at the Church of Notre Dame, he had received so many graces that he made an offering of himself to God. He was sixty-five at this time and was beginning to see in himself signs of aging, such as memory loss. Léonie was not strong enough to give him much help, but he knew that he could rely on Céline. For her devotion, he offered to take her to Paris, where she could pursue her artistic talent. She refused this kind offer and explained that she wanted only to become a nun. Whether Céline's decision, coming on top of the loss of three of his daughters already to Carmel, was too much for him is not known. But several days later, M. Martin disappeared. He was found a week later in Le Havre, confused as to how he had gotten there. Pauline said, "Many people held us responsible for this trouble." Thérèse was especially shaken because she was a "prisoner" when her beloved father needed her. Instead of the tears of old, she resolved to write cheerful and amusing letters to him and to Céline. This was particularly admirable because, at the time, Thérèse herself was having difficulty with prayer. She, who had always found her support in prayer, was experiencing dryness: the desert she had longed for as a child was now in her heart.

Thérèse Receives the Habit

After six months as a postulant, the community would review the aspirant and decide whether or not to welcome the new one into the community. In October the community voted that Thérèse would be welcomed. Unfortunately, M. Martin had had another attack in August and it was decided to delay the happy occasion until he was feeling better. The bishop was available in January, so it was shortly after her sixteenth birthday that Thérèse received the habit of a Carmelite sister.

The retreat she made in preparation for this event was just another hardship. Thérèse never seemed to get enough sleep. The dryness in prayer that she had been experiencing became worse. But she said, "If Jesus wants to sleep, why should I prevent Him?" Her reception of the habit represented to her the opportunity to make a complete gift of herself to her Spouse.

She wore a beautiful white velvet gown decorated with Alençon lace, donated by her father, and a crown of lilies given by her aunt. The whole family came to Mass. Her father, who looked better than he had for ages, walked her down the aisle to present her to the bishop. After Mass, the family accompanied Thérèse to the sacristy where sisters carrying lighted candles met her. The family could watch the rest of the ceremony through the grille.

At her entrance nine months before, she had taken the name Sister Thérèse of the Child Jesus. At this reception, she added "of the Holy Face." Now she donned her Carmelite habit of rough brown wool covered with a brown scapular and a white cloak. As a novice, her head was swathed in white. She wore a leather belt from which hung a large rosary. Woolen stockings and rope sandals completed her habit. Now strengthened, Thérèse desired more suffering, which was to come.

Reflection

Perhaps it is difficult to understand how the sufferings arising from a new diet, lack of sleep, life with incompatible strangers, worry about her father, and inability to find joy in prayer, all accepted joyfully, can lead to saintliness. This is the lesson St. Thérèse would have us learn. The life hidden in Jesus, accepting with joy whatever comes daily from his hands, is the way to perfection.

St. Thérèse, teach us to accept all with joy.

CHAPTER NINE

GROWING IN LOVE

Hide me in the shadow of your wings.
Psalm 17:8

To anyone observing Thérèse at this time, it would seem that all was peaceful and serene. With a quiet smile she went about her duties of sweeping the cloister walk, making communion hosts, and cleaning the refectory under the watchful eyes of Sister Agnès of Jesus. Her soul was at peace as a new bride of Our Lord. It was as if the boat carrying the Baby Jesus given her by Céline now carried Thérèse as well. Yet there were still the storms of daily living. Mother Marie continued to humiliate her. Sister Agnès frequently found fault with her work in the refectory. (This is somewhat ironic since Pauline had been the first to spoil Thérèse by doing everything for her.) The novice mistress was another source of trials because of her incessant chattering. At the same time, Thérèse's calm exterior was an annoyance to some of her less perfect companions. And then came another shattering blow.

M. Martin's Accelerating Illness

Just a month after he had accompanied Thérèse to the altar for her reception, M. Martin's mental instability worsened. He had been confined to bed, but suddenly he was seeing terrifying things. Céline found him waving a revolver in an effort to protect his family from the terrors of his visions. They had no choice. Uncle Isidore was summoned and it was decided to take M. Martin to a hospital in Caen that specialized in mental illness. He would remain there for three years. Léonie and Céline became boarders for a few months in a convent close to the hospital so that they could visit him frequently.

M. Martin had been well known and highly respected in the community, and it was humiliating that this illness had settled in his brain. All of the sisters were crushed at this development. And, of course, there was gossip. Had the sisters, particularly the youngest one, brought on this illness by entering Carmel and leaving their father almost alone in his advancing years? Thérèse saw in his suffering a likeness of the holy face of Jesus. Her father, too, was a man of sorrows.

Finally, after three years, M. Martin was brought back to Lisieux to visit his three daughters at Carmel. He was unable to speak, but just before he left, he looked up and gestured as if he were saying "in heaven." He could not return to Les Buissonnets because the house had been sold the year before, another sacrifice suffered by all the Martins.

Because of the suffering her father's agony caused her, Thérèse referred to the three years he spent in the hospital as "the most lovable, the most fruitful of my life; I wouldn't exchange them for all the ecstasies and revelations of the saints." Most saints rejoiced in ecstasies; instead, Thérèse rejoiced in all suffering as gifts she could offer to her Savior for the salvation of souls. She had learned the wisdom of becoming little, unknown, and unnoticed. As she wrote to her sister Marie, she wished only to be "truly hidden from all eyes." She said further, "I applied myself to practicing little virtues, not having the aptitude to practice great ones."

Convent Duties

When assignments of duties were given in Carmel, usually two were assigned with one in charge and the other as second or assistant. For example, Sister Agnès and Sister Thérèse were assigned to set the table in refectory and pour the water and beer. After the meal, they mended the tablecloths and cleaned the tables and floors. Sister Agnès was in charge and Thérèse was her assistant. In all her assignments, she was never in first place, always an assistant. And that was just the way Thérèse wanted it.

Some tasks the sisters did as a group, like laundry. Together they pounded, scrubbed, and soaked their habits and linens, grouped around a large tub. Later the garments were rinsed in outdoor tubs. Perhaps having her hands in this cold water so often weakened the already delicate Thérèse and made her susceptible to the tuberculosis that would soon end her life.

In her nine years in Carmel, Thérèse had many other assignments. One of her favorites was taking care of the sacristy because it was as close as she could get to being a priest. Handling the sacred vessels was a great privilege and one that she loved. Another task that she particularly took pleasure in was painting, which she had enjoyed as a child, painting scenes during summer vacations. When Pauline became prioress, she asked Thérèse to illuminate and paint religious pictures and church decorations. One summer Thérèse painted a fresco on the wall of a prayer room for the sick. This painting circled the tabernacle where the monstrance exposed the Blessed Sacrament on days of adoration.

When Sister Agnès became prioress, she assigned Thérèse to plan festivities for feast days, anniversaries, and professions. For these events she wrote poems and "entertainments." Her novice mistress said of her, "A mystic, a comic, she has everything going for her—she knows how to make you weep with devotion or die with laughter at recreation." Thérèse took on several writing projects. Two were plays about St. Joan of Arc. In 1894, all France was excited that Joan of Arc was to be called venerable, the first step on the way to canonization. She had long been a model for Thérèse, who read a new biography of Joan to write her play. Thérèse became writer, director, and main character in these dramas. In one production, she was in danger of being

actually burned as she stood at the stake like her mentor. Fortunately, the fire was doused in time.

At one point, Thérèse was forced into a leadership role. In 1891 a flu epidemic swept over Europe. The Lisieux convent was not spared. Three of the elderly nuns would die. Most of the others were confined to their beds. Thérèse was one of only three who were spared to care for the others. There were herbal teas to be brewed, prayers for the dying to be said, funerals to be prepared, and the choir grilles for Mass to be opened. Generally things were kept running, although the regular routine of community life was abandoned. Working tirelessly, Thérèse said, "The good Lord gave me many graces of strength at this time; I wonder now how I was able to do all that I did without fear." Impressed with her ability to cope, the priest superior, who had opposed her entrance a few years before, now acknowledged, "She is a great hope for the community."

Final Profession

It was customary that a novice like Thérèse would make her final vows of perpetual profession a year after receiving the habit. Once again, the priest superior refused to give this permission since Thérèse was only seventeen. He felt she was too young to take this important step. About this time, a Jesuit came to preach a retreat for the sisters. Thérèse confessed to him her desire to become a saint. Instead of supporting her aspiration, he condemned her for pride and presumption. Her reply was to quote Our Lord who had commanded, "Be perfect as your Heavenly Father is perfect." And she intended to achieve this perfection by accepting every opportunity to do small acts that would curb her self-love, such as accepting a scolding for breaking a vase that someone else had broken. She recognized that her impatience at the delay of her profession was just another sign of her self-love.

Finally, the bishop was consulted and September 8, 1890, the feast of the Nativity of the Blessed Virgin, was set for Thérèse's profession of vows. Accordingly, she made a private retreat beginning on August 28. Again, this was not a time of consolation for her. Instead she suffered more of the darkness and dryness that had become the norm for her prayer life. The suffering was so intense that while saying the Stations of the Cross the night before profession, she was terrorized with the thought that she had no vocation at all and was deceiving everyone. She needed the assurance of both her novice mistress and the prioress to calm her fears. However, on the day of her profession, she felt immersed in a "river of peace." Mother Marie wrote of her at this time, "This angelic seventeen-year-old has the judgment of a thirty-year-old, the religious perfection of an old and accomplished novice, and self-mastery. She is a perfect nun."

Two Deaths Endured with Peace

From the day in 1888 when Thérèse first entered Carmel, she had particular affection and reverence for Mother Geneviève of Sainte Thérèse, the founder of the

Carmel at Lisieux, who by that time was already an invalid. Mother Geneviève in turn recognized the treasure that Thérèse was to the convent. When darkness and aridity were overwhelming Thérèse, Mother Geneviève once offered her this comfort, "Serve God with peace and with joy; remember, my child, that our God is the God of peace." Mother Geneviève's death in late 1891 was the first that Thérèse had ever witnessed. Soon after Mother Geneviève died, Thérèse noticed a tear in the corner of her eye. She collected the tear and carried it with her, considering it the relic of a saint who would go immediately to heaven. A few nights later Thérèse dreamed that she saw Mother Geneviève writing her will and giving something to each Carmelite. To Thérèse she said three times, "I give you my heart."

A few years later, Thérèse had to endure another death—that of her father. Studying an image of Christ's holy face brought her the revelation that this suffering face was symbolic of her father's face. Then she remembered the vision she had seen in the garden of Les Buissonnets as a girl. Her dear father's face was hidden in his suffering. When it was suggested to her at her profession to ask for healing for him, she prayed only that God's will be done.

M. Martin's health had not improved since he returned from Caen. In the summer of 1894 he suffered first a stroke in May and then a heart attack in June. Céline, with the help of a manservant, was alone in caring for him, since Léonie had again entered the Visitation convent. On July 29, M. Martin died peacefully. He was a little more than seventy. All of the Martin sisters mourned deeply, although they felt he had gone immediately to heaven. Thérèse said, "God broke the bonds of His incomparable servant and called him to his eternal reward."

Céline's Decision

Even though Céline had cared for her father with love and devotion, she had also during this time attended social functions like the weddings of her friends. Thérèse, who knew of Céline's vow of chastity, was horrified that at one of these affairs her sister might participate in a waltz, a new and popular dance. Thérèse felt Céline was placing herself in a compromising situation. Céline had already received several proposals for marriage, all of which she had rejected. Now with the death of M. Martin, she was finally free to follow her vocation. But she had a decision to make. Father Pichon, who had been her spiritual advisor, wanted her to come to Canada to do active missionary work. Of course, the three Carmelites wanted their sister to join them. Uncle Isidore was at first reluctant to give his permission, and her cousin Jeanne was opposed to any religious vocation for Céline. Then, when she finally did decide to enter the Carmel at Lisieux, another obstacle presented itself.

St. Teresa of Avila had written, "No monastery is to have three sisters living together"—yet there were already three Martin sisters at Lisieux. Now a fourth? Naturally the priest superior supported the rule and opposed Céline's entrance. For one thing, in a small community, four from the same family could make life difficult for the others. The idea was not popular, and one of the sisters was particularly opposed to it. At Mass, Thérèse prayed for a sign. If M. Martin had gone immediately to heaven, let this sister agree to Céline's entry. After Mass, the sister approached Thérèse to tell her she no longer objected to Céline's coming to Carmel. Her entrance day was set for September 14, the feast of the Holy Cross.

Spiritual Influences

One of the great spiritual blessings that Thérèse received just a year after her profession was a retreat presented by Father Alexis Prou, a Franciscan. Most of the sisters at Lisieux were not happy with this choice of retreat master. Thérèse, however, finally found a priest who understood her soul. She said, "He launched me full sail on the waves of confidence and love which held such an attraction for me, but upon which I had not dared to venture." Father Prou brought her great peace and joy by explaining that her faults did not offend God and that, in fact, "God was very pleased" with her. But the quixotic Mother Marie, for whatever reason, forbade Thérèse to speak again to this priest. This was extremely difficult, but she remained obedient. She was never to see or talk to Father Prou again. This experience, and the fact that she did not hear from Father Pichon in Canada as often as she would have liked, made Thérèse decide that Jesus would be her spiritual director.

Another source of spiritual support came from reading. When Céline entered Carmel, she brought several things with her. Fortunately for the future, one was a camera, which she used to record convent events. Thérèse was not pleased with the picture taking but submitted gracefully. On the other hand she was delighted with a notebook that Céline brought with her in which she had written certain passages from the Old Testament. Thérèse had not studied the Old Testament, which at that time was not available to young sisters, so she was pleased to explore this notebook. There she found, "If anyone is a *very little one,* let him come to me" (Prov 9:4). She was delighted, since she knew herself to be that very little one.

Another passage that touched her deeply is from Isaiah 66: "As one whom a mother caresses, so will I comfort you." The Scriptures, both the Old and the New Testaments, were very important to her development. She carried a copy of the Gospels with her at all times and said, "It is especially the Gospels that sustain me during my hours of prayer, for in them I find what is necessary for my poor little soul."

Before her final profession she found great sustenance in the works of St. John of the Cross, the Carmelite who had written spiritual books to lead others to holiness. She kept in her cell his *Spiritual Canticle* and *Living Flame of Love.* She said, "At the age of seventeen and eighteen I had no other spiritual nourishment." At this time, St. John of the Cross was not widely read, even by Carmelites. Thérèse also found much to imitate in the works of St. Teresa of Avila, her mentor and mother in the spiritual life. She had read a biography of the saint before entering Carmel. Several of St. Teresa's sayings appear often in Thérèse's writing. Two examples are: "God alone suffices," and "I would give one thousand lives to save one soul."

Reflection

Thérèse would appear to many of her Carmelite sisters as an ordinary, good person. Certainly they saw in her love of Our Lord only what should be expected of a good Carmelite. What was not apparent superficially was Thérèse's relish of suffering for love, a suffering that she hoped would be used to somehow "fill up" the suffering of Christ. As she matured in her spiritual life, she would turn all her pains and sorrows to him, working "solely for the salvation of souls."

St. Thérèse, show us the way to relish
our sufferings for love.

CHAPTER TEN

LIVING THE "LITTLE WAY"

Search me, O God, and know my heart;
test me and know my thoughts...
and lead me in the way everlasting.
Psalm 139:23–24

At the time of Thérèse's first communion, Marie had taught her the importance of little actions done with love, and Thérèse had never forgotten the lesson. Doing small things with immense love would be the foundation of Thérèse's spiritual message. Since her early days in Carmel, she had been dispensing this message by means of letters, especially to her sister Céline and her cousin Marie Guérin, who would both later enter Carmel. Her plays, poetry, and autobiography continued to support her teaching as Thérèse herself matured in her understanding of the "Little Way" that she would teach the world.

The child who was once too proud and stubborn to pick up a coin would use her strong will to conquer herself, the most difficult battle we all face. The child who once greedily wanted to "choose all" would use this trait to choose and accept all that was offered to her by her Divine Spouse, saying "I don't want to be a *saint by halves.*" The child who suffered for years from scruples would teach others how to avoid this devastating spiritual disease by trusting in God's mercy. The child who was once unhappy to be outside her family circle would reach out without fear to the whole world to teach her "Little Way." First she would suffer and love from her lowly position in Carmel, but at the end of her twenty-four years, she would rise to the heights of sanctity. All the while her outward life was so unremarkable that when she died, one of the Carmelite sisters said it would be difficult to find something to say about Thérèse for the death notice that would be sent to other Carmelite monasteries.

Continued Suffering

As we have seen, Thérèse's nature was extremely sensitive. The loss of her mother, Zélie, and her "second" mother, Pauline, had caused her much suffering. Later Pauline would realize the pain she had caused the young Thérèse by leaving and try to compensate for it. Being separated from her beloved father, who had loved her with a mother's love, had also been painful for Thérèse. Further, she keenly felt the suffering he endured before his death.

Following Pauline and Marie to Carmel did not recreate for Thérèse the loving atmosphere of Les Buissonnets where she had flourished. Both of her sisters took pains not to treat her as the "Little Flower," or even as the "child" of the convent, although for many of her nine years there, she was. Her two older sisters were there for loving support, but Thérèse was expected to find her own way, as she did. Also, as noted before, Mother Marie, who had shown Thérèse great love before her entrance, would often treat her harshly. Nevertheless, Thérèse continued to love her as she did her blood sisters. And this was the cause of added suffering.

Mother Marie may well have anticipated remaining the superior at Carmel for her entire life, but when Thérèse was twenty, Sister Agnès (Pauline) was elected prioress. This was apparently a blow to Mother Marie's pride. And instead of being a support for the new prioress, she made things difficult. Thérèse was caught between the two "mothers," both of whom she loved. Mother Marie was now assigned to be the novice mistress with Thérèse as her assistant. Thérèse soon learned the difficult skill of walking the tightrope stretched between the two women so that she could please the one without displeasing the other.

Novices Assigned to Thérèse's Care

One of the first souls to come under Thérèse's guidance was Sister Martha. She had been orphaned early in her life and had entered Carmel just a few months before Thérèse; consequently they were in the novitiate together. Sister Martha, who was to become a lay sister, early on grew too attached to Mother Marie, probably because she had known little of her own mother's love. Thérèse observed this and knew that this attachment would stand in the way of Sister Martha's development. Thérèse risked the anger of Sister Martha, who was known for her fierce temper, and also risked Mother Marie's anger if she heard about it. After prayer and consultation with Sister Agnès, Thérèse determined to speak to Sister Martha. With tenderness and tact, she explained that true love sacrifices itself as it seeks the good of the other. The novice understood and recognized that this natural love for her prioress was standing in the way of her own spiritual growth.

Later, as assistant to the novice mistress, Thérèse was asked to look after a young woman who had come to the convent from Paris. Sister Marie of the Trinity had left a previous Carmel because of her health, but perhaps other problems as well. She was apparently highly emotional and flighty and was soon termed "The Little Mischief" because she seemed to attract trouble. She said of Thérèse, "Since she was always correcting my faults, I would have liked to find some imperfection in her, but I never could." As Sister Marie of the Trinity, schooled by Thérèse, grew in her own spiritual life, the two became close spiritual friends. Thérèse explained to her: "People must not think that our 'little way' is a restful one, full of sweetness and consolation. It is quite the opposite. To offer oneself as a victim to love is to offer oneself to suffering because love lives only on sacrifice."

As assistant novice mistress, Thérèse was to oversee the spiritual growth of five novices, four of whom were older than she. On most days she met with them at 2:30

for a half hour to explain the Rule and customs, to answer questions, and to give advice. This required great tact and fortitude, but Thérèse relied entirely on her Lord, admitting to him, "I am too little to nourish your children." Céline and her cousin Marie Guérin were part of this group. It would have been easy for Thérèse to have treated these two with special love. Instead they both declared her strict. Thérèse said of dealing with the novices, "There are some I have to take by the scruff of the neck, and others by the tip of their wings."

Two Missionary Priests Assigned to Her Care

A young seminarian wrote to Carmel asking for a sister to pray especially for him. His request was that she would pray for the salvation of his soul and, further, by her prayers and sacrifices help him in his missionary work to save many souls. Mother Agnès committed his appeal to Thérèse. She was delighted because two of her most fervent desires were being satisfied. She had always wanted a priest-brother, and she also longed to be a missionary. Later, after Mother Marie's reelection, she also assigned another seminarian to Thérèse's spiritual care, although Thérèse was at first reluctant to accept the additional responsibility. He came to Carmel to celebrate his first Mass and shortly after left for China as a missionary. Thérèse doubled her prayers and sacrifices. She kept in touch with both priests through letters. To one she sent a message, which summed up her feelings for both, saying that she hoped he would be "not only a good missionary, but ablaze with the love of God and of souls." She also asked for prayers for herself because she felt that, by being united in the work of these missionary priests, she was fulfilling the will of Teresa of Avila who wished to "give a thousand lives to save one soul."

Writing Her Autobiography, **Story of a Soul**

Thérèse's path to sanctity is best explained by herself in her autobiography, a manuscript written in three parts and addressed to three different people: her sister Pauline as Mother Agnès, her sister Marie, and Mother Marie. Each part was written not to please herself, but at the express request of the person to whom it was addressed.

The autobiography was begun one evening during recreation in 1895. Thérèse was entertaining Marie and Pauline with stories of their lives at Les Buissonnets. Marie remarked that Thérèse should be asked to write her memories for them. Pauline complied and, as Mother Agnès, placed Thérèse under obedience to write this memoir. Finding time in her day was not easy, but Thérèse prepared the manuscript in time to present it to her sister for her feast day. Her story covered her life up until shortly after her entrance to Carmel. (Thérèse presented the manuscript to Mother Agnès in January, 1896. Mother Agnès would not find time to read it for months, but Thérèse never questioned her about it, as if this work were of no concern to her.)

THÉRÈSE OF LISIEUX

The next section of the book was written at the request of her sister Marie, who asked Thérèse during her private retreat in September 1896 to explain in writing her "Little Way." This manuscript contains the core of her teaching. Because of her great love of her Savior, Thérèse desired to serve him in every way possible as warrior, priest, apostle, doctor, and martyr. But she recognized the impossibility of that desire and wrote: "O Jesus, my Love....My vocation, at last I have found it....MY VOCATION IS LOVE." Her love for Jesus and the church, her mother, led her to recall from the words of St. John of the Cross that *"the smallest act of PURE LOVE is of more value to her than all other works together."*

When Mother Agnès finally read the manuscript given her by Thérèse, she realized that Thérèse's life in Carmel was barely described. By that time the always-frail Thérèse had fallen ill and was growing weaker, and her death seemed certain. But Mother Marie had been elected prioress again. Mother Agnès could no longer place Thérèse under obedience to complete her story and getting Mother Marie to make the request required tact and delicacy. A clever strategy was needed. Mother Agnès explained to Mother Marie that they really had no record of Thérèse's life in Carmel. Consequently they would have very little resource for the brief biography to be sent to other Carmels at Thérèse's death. Mother Agnès then suggested that Mother Marie ask Thérèse to describe her life in Carmel. In June Mother Marie requested the final manuscript of *The Story of a Soul* be written. Thérèse would die three months later in September.

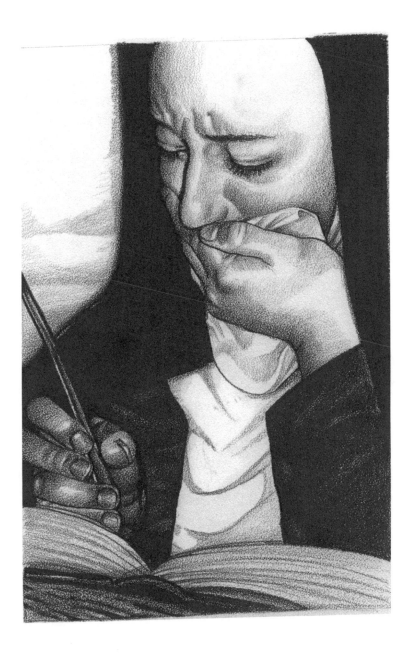

THÉRÈSE OF LISIEUX

The Act of Merciful Love

Even though a priest had rebuked Thérèse after confessing her desire to be a saint, the desire remained buried deep in her heart. She had learned from reading the spiritual writings of John of the Cross that God does not inspire desires that cannot be fulfilled. She knew that she could not imitate the "great" saints with their heroic actions, ecstasies, and visions. But she reasoned that God's garden is filled with many flowers: roses, lilies, and the little white flower that her father had given her along with his permission to enter Carmel. She would be that "Little Flower." She wrote, "Perfection consists in doing His will, in being what He wills us to be." She determined not to allow "one little sacrifice to escape, not one look, one word, profiting by all the smallest things and doing them through love."

Previously, several of the Carmelites, including Mother Geneviève, had offered themselves as "victims of justice"; that is, they offered themselves to God to suffer the punishments deserved by sinners, thus to make reparation for their sins. This seemed too grand an offering for Thérèse to make. But on the feast of Holy Trinity during Mass, she was inspired. She would offer herself as "sacrificial victim to merciful love." Permission to make this offering of herself was needed. So with Sister Geneviève (Céline), she approached Mother Agnès for permission.

Given permission, Thérèse rushed to her cell to write out the offering that she and Céline would pronounce together two days later. They knelt in front of the statue of the Blessed Virgin who had smiled at Thérèse so long ago. The offering begins:

> O My God! Most Blessed Trinity, I desire to *love* You and make You *loved*, to work for the glory of Holy Church by saving souls on earth and liberating those suffering in purgatory. I desire to accomplish Your will perfectly and to reach the degree of glory You have prepared for me in Your Kingdom. I desire, in a word, to be a saint, but I feel my helplessness and I beg You, O my God! to be Yourself my *Sanctity!*

After Mother Agnès submitted the offering to a theologian for approval, Thérèse shared it, hoping others might participate in the graces she received as a result of her offering. She prayed, "O Jesus! Why can't I tell all little souls how unspeakable is Your condescension?…I feel that if you found a soul weaker and littler than mine, which is impossible, You would be pleased to grant it still greater favors, provided it abandoned itself with total confidence to Your infinite Mercy."

Reflection

Many thousands of people have since made this offering as they attempted to follow Thérèse's "Little Way." They have discovered, though it may be little, "the way" is difficult. To be constantly attentive to God's presence, accepting all that comes from his hands, and finding ways to stifle self-love, is challenging work. These small sacrifices offered each day to fill up, as St. Paul suggests, what is wanting in the sufferings of Christ, are graces Thérèse has modeled for us. Not because Christ's suffering is insufficient, but because God, in his infinite love for us, allows us to play a small part in the work of our redemption.

St. Thérèse, open our hearts to follow in your
"Little Way."

CHAPTER ELEVEN

ALL IS DARKNESS

And now my soul is poured out within me;
days of affliction have taken hold of me.

Job 30:16

One of Thérèse's sufferings not previously described was the cold she endured at Carmel. Only the room where the sisters gathered for recreation had a fireplace. All the other rooms—chapel, refectory, cells, and cloisters—were unheated, and each winter Thérèse suffered what she called "the hell of cold." Thérèse did little to protect herself from it and it frequently brought on a sore throat and chest pains years before her death. When the doctor was called to examine her, he determined that the sore throat was the result of her speaking too often to the novices. This did little to cure Thérèse's real complaint of tuberculosis, but it did lead her to more use of her pen for letters, plays, and poems.

In the late nineteenth century tuberculosis was little understood and was to the world then something like AIDS is today. There was no cure; it frequently attacked the young; and people were frightened of it. The advance of the disease was no doubt hastened by the austerity of life at Carmel, with its restricted diet, limited sleep, and lack of modern hygiene. Outside the convent, people afflicted were often shunted away from the family. In Carmel, they were prayed for but were generally given little in the way of adequate medical attention.

Holy Thursday, 1896

On April 3, 1896, Thérèse had stayed up until midnight praying in the choir. When she finally reached her cell, she would have less than six hours to sleep before everyone was called to prayer. It didn't matter; she was full of energy and enthusiasm for the Holy Days. Shortly after she had put out her lamp and laid down, she felt a rush, "a bubbling stream" in her mouth. It would be against the Rule to relight her lamp, so she just used her handkerchief to stem the flow and would look in the morning. She was filled with joy as she was sure that this was a sign that her Divine Spouse was coming for her soon.

It's important to see Thérèse's joy at her illness not with the eyes of the modern materialist but with the understanding of one whose entire being was centered on heaven as our eternal home. She was joyful not simply to have pain, but at the idea of soon being united with Jesus, whom she loved with her whole heart. As a child she had chosen all. Now at twenty-four, she was not choosing, she was abandoning herself to her coming death because it meant a real union with the Jesus she loved without reservation.

In the morning, she discovered that she had, indeed, hemorrhaged during the night. The thought that she might be spitting up blood on Good Friday, the day that Jesus shed his blood for all, gave her increased joy. One of the events of the day was a general talk by Mother Marie on charity, ending with the sisters embracing one another as they forgave each other's faults. When Thérèse embraced Mother Marie, she whispered her news, telling Mother Marie of her "hope" and "happiness" and asked her to keep the secret.

Thérèse said later, "The hope of going to heaven… transported me with joy." Filled with energy, she concluded the day by washing windows. Sister Martha saw her pale face and offered to take her place, but Thérèse insisted on completing the task herself. That night she suffered another hemorrhage. This time her superiors were concerned and the doctor was called. He questioned the fully clothed Thérèse closely through the grille. By leaning his head through the grille to examine her, he discovered a swollen gland in her neck. He decided that the bleeding must have come from a blood vessel that had burst in her throat and prescribed some simple medication. Medications did not matter because Thérèse was filled with joy at the certainty that she would soon be going to her heavenly home.

Darkness Soon Reigns

"At this time," Thérèse wrote, "I was enjoying such a living faith, such a clear faith, that the thought of heaven made up all my happiness." Soon, however, her joy disappeared, and she was filled with the darkness that Our Lord sometimes gives to his friends to test their faith. She began to be tempted to doubt herself, her "Little Way," and her offering made to love. Even the existence of heaven was a matter of temptation to doubt for her. She feared that all that she had done was nothing and for nothing. To overcome these temptations required many acts of faith.

In *The Story of a Soul*, she wrote to Mother Marie of this trying time: "The image I wanted to give you of the darkness that obscures my soul is…imperfect." But she feared writing more to describe this total and utter darkness of faith lest she "blaspheme." She fought her doubts by doing as she had long trained herself to do—casting her turmoil and her fears on Jesus. And in spite of the loss of joy and being overcome with temptations against faith, she could say with the psalmist, *"You have given me DELIGHT, O Lord, in ALL your doings."* Somehow in all this misery, she recognized that the Lord had not given her this trial until she was able to bear it. While these terrible interior battles were raging, no one among her companions was aware of what she was suffering. She was still writing and speaking of the joy to be found in loving God and appeared to be enjoying his consolations.

A Prophetic Dream

Thérèse was not given to dreams, particularly dreams of a spiritual nature, but one she had in May of 1896 brought her a moment of light in the midst of darkness.

In the dream she saw three Carmelites. One she recognized as Mother Anne of Jesus, the friend and companion of St. Teresa of Avila and St. John of the Cross. Thérèse felt great affection and consolation coming to her from the dream and dared to ask the question that was uppermost in her mind, "Will he come to get me soon?"

Mother Anne assured her, "Yes, soon…I promise you."

Thérèse was so delighted with this answer she dared to ask another question which, given the turmoil of faith she was suffering, was very important to her: "Is he pleased with me?" The answer came back that he was very pleased, and Thérèse, though it was only a dream, had a few moments of peace.

Roses Begin to Fall

One of the promises Thérèse would make before her death was that she would send from heaven a shower of roses to those who needed or asked for favors. We already mentioned the two priest-brothers Thérèse was praying for. One of them, Father Roulland, was in China, and had written about the need for sisters in the Carmel at Saigon. Thérèse was eager to answer this call, with her lifelong desire to be a missionary, but her health was already failing. She wrote to Father Roulland, "Good-bye brother—distance can never separate our souls, even death will only make our union stronger. If I go to heaven soon, I shall ask Jesus' permission to visit you in Su-Chuen and we shall continue our apostolate together." She already clearly saw her assignment as a heavenly missionary. She might refer to herself as Jesus' ball, a little reed, a child, a bird, a flower, a grain of sand or dust, everything little, but at the same time she seemed to know she would soon perform great wonders from heaven.

At the community retreat later that year, the priest suggested that she carry the Creed with her always. The priest advised that this would strengthen her in dealing with the terrible temptations of faith that were so troubling to her, even while she was composing her description of her "Little Way." Thérèse took his advice. She wrote the Creed in her own blood, folded the paper, and carried it in a book of the Gospels, which always remained close to her. She said of this time, "I believe I have made more acts of faith in the past year than I have made in my whole life."

On the occasion of Mother Agnès' feast, shortly after Thérèse's twenty-fourth birthday, she wrote the poem "My Joy" for her. The lines "and I redouble my love/ when he hides from my faith" show that Thérèse's darkness continued, and her solution was to intensify her love. And yet no one around her recognized the depth of her suffering.

She began again a habit from her childhood of spreading the petals of flowers for her Lord and involved the novices in this summer evening ritual. They would gather rose petals from the garden and strew them at the feet of the cloister crucifix. Thérèse declared that the petals that touched the image of the crucified Lord would acquire great value for the salvation of souls. She explained that the petals were also symbolic of the acts

of love they had all offered during the day. The petals can also be seen as a foreshadowing of the shower of roses that Thérèse would send from heaven to lead other little souls to greater love of God.

Final Sickness and Death

After the two hemorrhages of Holy Week, Thérèse did not cease carrying out her daily assignments. Throughout the rest of the year she continued to instruct the novices and to write letters, poems, and entertainments for special occasions when she was asked to do so. Her sisters, Pauline, Marie, and Céline, although they noticed her pale face, had no idea of the extent of Thérèse's weakness. Mother Marie had kept Thérèse's secret.

As winter approached, the doctor ordered that Thérèse should receive a rubdown with a horsehair glove and a hot mustard plaster on her chest. Neither of these remedies would do much for the disease that was consuming her, but they did offer more opportunities for suffering. Mother Marie, who was prioress at this time, also ordered a heater for her cell and allowed her an extra hour of sleep. With wry humor, Thérèse commented on these extras, saying that the great saints went to heaven with their penances, but that she would go with her foot warmer.

Lent 1897 brought more weakness and in letters and poems Thérèse continued to warn others both of her approaching death and of her promise to be with them and to do good for them from heaven. She was exhausted and constantly racked with coughs, which further exhausted her. By May, she was relieved of all duties. She no longer needed to attend religious exercises, recreations, and common work.

At Mother Marie's request after Mother Agnès' suggestion, in June she began to write the last section of *The Story of a Soul.* She would only have the strength to write for a short time. In July the pencil, which she found easier to handle than a pen, fell from her hand. Her last written words were "I go to Him with confidence and love." Thus she affirmed again that total trust in God's mercy and a total offering of self in love was the heart of the "Little Way."

This was not the end of her messages for the world. Fortunately, since April, she and Mother Agnès had conversed almost daily, and Pauline had recorded her sayings in a "Yellow Notebook." Céline, Marie, and their cousin Marie also collected and recorded Thérèse's words during their visits with her in the last months of her life. These exchanges have been lovingly collected and published in *St. Thérèse of Lisieux: Her Last Conversations.*

Thérèse was taken to the infirmary at the beginning of July. Waiting eagerly for death for over a year, since Holy Week of 1896, she was to embrace the suffering of her last days with her usual trust and enthusiasm. Today patients would receive sedatives to relieve their distress. Thérèse received nothing though she could not breathe and was actually suffocating with the disease. On the last day, Mother Agnès recorded these words spoken to Mother Marie: "I am not sorry for delivering myself up to Love....Never would I have believed it was possible to suffer so much! never! never! I cannot explain this except by the ardent desires I have had to save souls."

The community, which had been assembled for Thérèse's last moments, was dismissed. At first afraid this was a sign that she was still not going to die, Thérèse struggled to accept his will and said, "I would not want to suffer for a shorter time." Shortly after, looking at the crucifix she was holding, Thérèse said, "Oh! I love him!...My God...I love you!..." The sisters, who had been hastily recalled, saw her face, which had been blue from lack of oxygen, regain some color. A smile wreathed her face as she offered him her last breath.

Reflection

In spite of all the suffering, both physical and mental, of her last months, Thérèse remained firmly rooted in Our Lord. She teaches us that no matter what our sins may be, if we will but trust in him with a child's complete faith and have the desire to love him with our whole hearts, he will reward us with a place in one of the many mansions of heaven. And if we ask her, Thérèse will work tirelessly on our behalf rewarding us with a shower of roses.

St. Thérèse, help us to increase our faith and trust in him.

CHAPTER TWELVE

THÉRÈSE'S NEW LIFE
AS A HEAVENLY MISSIONARY

My heaven will be spent on earth up until the end of the world.
Yes, I want to spend my heaven in doing good on earth.
                                              Last Conversations

Thérèse's *The Story of a Soul* began an avalanche as
the Lord fulfilled her desire to spend her time in
heaven working. The list of the graces she has shed on
the world would fill another book. John Paul II noted
in his address proclaiming her a Doctor of the Universal Church that the reception of her book, her life, and
her work "was quick, universal, and constant."

In 1898, Mother Agnès edited and published 2000
copies of *Histoire D'une Ame* on the first anniversary of
Thérèse's death. Uncle Isidore paid for this publication. The book was sent to Carmel monasteries and to a
few friends. Like the birds that Thérèse so loved, the
book took flight and was passed from hand to hand.
For the next five years the book was reprinted each

year. Today millions of copies of the book have been published, and it has been translated into more than fifty languages.

Soon a flood of mail came to the Lisieux Carmel. Thérèse had said that after her death her sisters would find consolation in the mailbox. The mail began as a trickle of a few daily letters. In just the few years before her beatification it swelled to between five hundred and a thousand a day. Today, more than a hundred years later, an average of fifty letters a day come daily to Carmel.

Pilgrimages to Thérèse's burial site in Lisieux began almost immediately after the publication of the *Histoire.* A notable early pilgrim was a young Scottish priest. He had read Thérèse's story, and after a visit to Lourdes in 1903 stopped at Lisieux to propose to the sisters there that the process for canonization should be begun. Mother Marie's response was that if Thérèse should be canonized, so should all Carmelites. And she was not the only one to question Thérèse's sanctity. Her own sister Léonie and the Guérins also resisted the move for beatification. They considered saints to be peculiar people while their Thérèse was quite ordinary. Léonie was soon to reenter the Visitation convent as Thérèse had predicted earlier. Also as Thérèse had predicted, Léonie would take Thérèse as part of her religious name, and this time she would remain in the convent until death.

Even though postulants were begging to be accepted at Lisieux because of Thérèse, the Carmelites were still so unimpressed with this "ordinary" sister they did not begin to save the mail describing blessings and cures until 1909 when a priest suggested they should do so. But meanwhile, others were also asking that the process be begun. In 1907, Pius X, in a private audience, declared Thérèse "the greatest saint of modern times." It was also in 1909 that the first recorded miracle occurred (although this was not one later considered by the church in the beatification process). A four-year-old blind girl had been brought by her mother to Thérèse's tomb. Her sight was restored instantaneously.

Process for Beatification Moves Quickly

In January of 1910, just thirteen years after Thérèse's death, the process of beatification was begun. The church, which usually takes hundreds of years to canonize someone, moved swiftly for Thérèse because so many people clamored for it. One cardinal close to the Holy Father declared that it was important to move the process quickly before Thérèse was declared a saint by popular acclaim, as happened with the early saints. Thirty-nine witnesses, including nine Carmelites, were called to testify to Thérèse's heroic virtues. Her body was exhumed, placed in a lead coffin, and moved to a vault. Collecting and weighing testimony can consume a great deal of time, and World War I interrupted the process. Thérèse's work, however, was not interrupted. Soldiers on both sides of the conflict reported her intercession on their behalf.

Two miracles were selected from among hundreds. In the first, a religious sister, a Daughter of the Cross, was cured of a hemorrhaging ulcer that had proved impossible to treat until Thérèse interceded. In the second, a seminarian who prayed to Thérèse was cured of serious pulmonary problems. Three doctors authenticated these cures. Pius XI thus declared her beatified on April 29, 1923. He himself had particular devotion to Thérèse who, he felt, brought a message of great importance to modern times.

Two more miracles would be required for her canonization. A young sister had been suffering intense pain for ten years from an infection in her knee that had spread to her spine. In 1923 she was encouraged to attend a novena to St. Thérèse. The sister had tried every remedy for her crippling infirmity without success. So during the novena, she had been praying for others and was not anticipating or asking for a cure for herself. But again, as three doctors would attest, she was completely cured.

The second miracle involved a young woman who had been suffering from tuberculosis and related problems for four years. Again, she had been given every possible medical treatment without success. She traveled to Lourdes seeking a cure but found none. Later she went with a small group of pilgrims to Lisieux. While kneeling at Thérèse's tomb, she was instantly healed.

In 1925, just two years after her beatification, Pius XI canonized Thérèse. In his homily he called upon Christians to imitate her spiritual childhood, urging those present (and there were more than 500,000 who had come to Rome for this occasion) to become like "children" as Our Lord had exhorted.

Honors Multiply

In 1927, St. Thérèse of the Child Jesus and the Holy Face was named patron of the universal missions along with St. Francis Xavier. This honor was unusual for one who had never stepped outside the walls of the Carmel of Lisieux, but it fulfilled Thérèse's desire to be a missionary. In 1944, Pius XII named her, along with her beloved Joan of Arc, patroness of France. Earlier, as cardinal, Pius XII had dedicated the Basilica of Lisieux, built to accommodate the millions of pilgrims who flocked there. Thousands of other churches, eight cathedrals, and five minor basilicas are now dedicated to her. Many religious congregations and seminaries have St. Thérèse as their patroness, as do the Catholic Worker Movement and *Deus Caritas,* the Theresian Secular Institute. This Institute, approved in 1979, is for laity to live the gospel in the spirit of St. Thérèse. In Cairo, even the Muslims gave a basilica to the "little saint of Allah" to thank her for all the favors they received from her. But the greatest honor was still to come.

Before 1970, no woman had been named a Doctor of the Church, not even after Vatican Council II, where the influence of St. Thérèse was felt in the proceedings. Pius XI had been encouraged to honor St. Thérèse with this title, but he apparently felt the church was not ready. In 1970 Paul VI named Saints Teresa of Avila and Catherine of Siena Doctors of the Church. Finally, in 1997, on the occasion of the centenary of St. Thérèse's death, her long-ago wish to be a "doctor" was fulfilled. At that time, John Paul II confirmed Thérèse, the youngest doctor saint, as "a teacher of the spiritual life with a doctrine both spiritual and profound." He said further, "She has made the Gospel shine appealingly in our time; she had the mission of making the Church, the Mystical Body of Christ, known and loved; she helped to heal souls of the rigors and fears of Jansenism, which tended to stress God's justice rather than his divine mercy." John Paul II felt that as a young person she is "particularly effective in illumining the paths of young people, who must be the leaders and witnesses of the Gospel to the new generations."

Her relics have traveled to twenty-two countries and been venerated by millions. A Canadian deacon commented, when more than two million Canadians flocked to honor her relics, "Thérèse's greatest miracle is still ongoing—the ability of such a simple and short life to bring inspiration and comfort to millions."

How then can one follow the "Little Way" that Thérèse walked? Trying to describe her way in a few words is a little like trying to pour Niagara Falls into a thimble! Her way is strongly based on her reading and thinking about scripture. That makes it deceptively simple, and perhaps overly familiar. Thérèse found the heart of scriptural passages, made them her own, and then shared them with us. Many interpretations and directions have been written to light the way for us, and it seems fitting here to look at a few of the suggestions St. Thérèse has given us.

Her first insistence is on the importance of loving God. Her love was so intense that she hungered for many vocations: to be a warrior, a priest, an apostle, a doctor, a martyr. She found the answer to her conflicting desires by meditating on the twelfth chapter of St.

Paul's First Epistle to the Corinthians, where he speaks of the many different members of Christ's body, the church. After reading this, Thérèse described in capital letters her understanding that "LOVE COMPRISED ALL VOCATIONS, THAT LOVE WAS EVERYTHING, THAT IT EMBRACED ALL TIMES AND PLACES.... IN A WORD, THAT IT WAS ETERNAL." And then she exclaimed: "At last I have found it....MY VOCATION IS LOVE." A few sentences later, she continued with a favorite theme of hers, "I am only a child, powerless and weak, and yet it is my weakness that gives me the boldness to offer myself."

Her second suggestion came from the recognition of her own childlikeness. She found support in St. Matthew's Gospel for this important element of the "Little Way." The scene is of the disciples questioning Jesus about who is the greatest in heaven. Jesus calls a child before them and says, "Unless you change and become like children, you will never enter the kingdom of God. Whoever becomes humble like this child is the greatest in the kingdom of heaven." Thérèse recognized, better than the disciples, that a child needs a father, and so she turned with loving trust to her heavenly Father.

Trust is also an important element of the "Little Way." For Thérèse, trust meant acceptance of all that happened to her. Just as a tiny child she had chosen all in her sister's offering of ribbons and bits of material, now she would choose all that her heavenly Father offered. She accepted with love her earthly father's tormented illness, the daily trials of convent living, and her own final suffering.

A child who loves and trusts the father is always searching for small ways in which to please him. Remembering our own childhoods helps us see how to do this. A child finds a flower or even a pretty stone and brings it to the father. With a loving smile the father accepts the small token with tenderness and takes the child in his arms for a warm hug. With this in mind, Thérèse taught her novices to collect rose petals to represent the acts of love and sacrifice of each day. The petals were then placed before the crucifix in the convent garden. What can we offer? A sharp retort that is suppressed, a bit of gossip not repeated, a treat passed up—small actions like these help us to follow Thérèse's way.

Thérèse shows us that our acts of love and sacrifice, small and insignificant though they may be, will be accepted lovingly by God if they are offered with love. Not only will these small tokens be accepted, but God will not be outdone in generosity and will reward the imperfect giver with additional graces. In a prayer to Jesus, Thérèse wrote, "I feel that if You found a soul weaker and littler than mine, which is impossible, You would be pleased to grant it still greater favors, provided it abandoned itself with total confidence to Your Infinite Mercy."

Probably most of us cannot claim, as Thérèse did, never to have knowingly offended God since the age of three. But this only puts us in a stronger position to ask for and receive favors if we are willing to become a true child, filled with love for and complete trust in the Father. Thérèse has asked Jesus to cast a "Divine

Glance" upon those willing to become childlike in their love and trust.

Reflection

One of Thérèse's sayings was "The soul gets exactly what it expects from God." Have we expected enough from our loving Savior, who will give us all things if only we will become as little children? Loving with the innocent faith of a child, trusting in his infinite mercy as a child trusts its father, is all that we are asked to do. If we can abandon ourselves to his love, he can do wonders for us, as Thérèse has shown us.

*St. Thérèse, teach us to become his children
and not be afraid to ask.*

BIBLIOGRAPHY

Autobiography of St. Thérèse of Lisieux. Trans. Ronald Knox. New York: P. J. Kennedy & Sons, 1962.

Autobiography of St. Thérèse of Lisieux: Story of a Soul. Trans. John Clarke, O.C.D. Third edition. Washington, D.C.: ICS Publications, 1996.

Bouyer, Louis. *Women Mystics.* Trans. Anne Englund Nash. San Francisco: Ignatius Press, 1993.

Catholic Women's Devotional Bible. New Revised Standard Version. Catholic edition. Grand Rapids, Mich.: Zondervan Publishing, 2000.

Céline: Sister Geneviève of the Holy Face, Sister and Witness of Saint Thérèse of the Child Jesus. Trans. Carmelite Sisters of the Eucharist, Colchester, Conn. San Francisco: Ignatius Press, 1997.

Chalon, Jean. *Thérèse of Lisieux: A Life of Love.* Trans. Anne Collier Rehill. Liguori, Mo.: Liguori Publications, 1997.

De Meester, Conrad, O.C.D. *I Offer Myself to Your Love: Commentary on Thérèse of Lisieux's Offering to Merciful Love.* Editions du Signe. Trans. Susan Conroy, 2000.

Experiencing Saint Thérèse Today. Ed. John Sullivan, O.C.D. Washington, D.C.: ICS Publications, 1990.

THÉRÈSE OF LISIEUX

Foley, Marc, O.C.D. *The Love That Keeps Us Sane: Living the Little Way of St. Thérèse of Lisieux.* New York/ Mahwah, N.J.: Paulist Press, 2000.

Gaucher, Guy. *The Story of a Life: St. Thérèse of Lisieux.* San Francisco: HarperCollins, 1993.

Hallett, Elaine. "To Die of Love," *New Oxford Review.* September 2001, pp. 44–45.

John Paul II. "Divini Amoris Scientia," http://www.catholicforum.com/saints/stt0200r.htm.

Johnson, Vernon. *Spiritual Childhood: The Spirituality of St. Thérèse of Lisieux.* San Francisco: Ignatius Press, 1953.

Nickerson, Colin. "A Saint's Canadian Processional," *Boston Sunday Globe.* December 16, 2001.

Saint Thérèse of Lisieux: Her Last Conversations. Trans. John Clarke, O.C.D. Washington, D.C.: ICS Publications, 1977.

Saint Thérèse of Lisieux: Her Life, Times, and Teaching. Gen. Ed. Conrad De Meester. Washington, D.C.: ICS Publications, 1997.

St. Thérèse of Lisieux by Those Who Knew Her: Testimonies from the Process of Beatification. Ed. and Trans. Christopher O'Mahony. Dublin: Veritas Publications, 1975.

Thérèse: Living on Love. Narrated by Joe Campanella. Ft. Collins, Col.: Ignatius Press, Frank Frost Productions, 2000.

Werning, David Hugh. "From Separation to Union: Thérèse's Journey to God," *Spiritual Life,* Spring 2000, pp. 24–35.